"We don't like to think of death. In fact, we're enslaved by the fear of it. In these devotions, Elyse Fitzpatrick teaches us how to remember death without fear—by remembering the one who tasted death so that we never will. *Friend of Sinners* is a lavish feast for your Lenten fast."

ERIC SCHUMACHER, Author, *The Good Gift of Weakness*

"Endorsements must be brief, which means I cannot share all the ways this devotional impacted me, but let me just say there were many moments when it was impossible to read Elyse's depiction of Jesus with a dry eye. You will be impacted again and again in unforgettable ways as the season of Lent takes on deeper meaning with each page. I will be sharing this with many."

ELIZA HUIE, Author; Counselor; Speaker

"I love how Elyse kindles our imaginations enough to enable us to step into the sandals of those we've perhaps glossed over during our Bible readings. As you read this book, I'd wager you might find yourself pausing to pray, repent, and sometimes just say, 'Wow!' I know I did."

QUINA ARAGON, Author, *Love Has a Story*

"In a time of immense loneliness, Elyse's devotional is a welcome return to a season that connects us to Christ and each other. *Friend of Sinners* gently invites us to the rhythms of our faith. I look forward to sharing it with others during this Lenten season."

CHRIS MOLES, Founder, PeaceWorks

"Elyse masterfully guides us through the somber, reflective season of Lent while always reminding us that Easter Sunday is coming. Each devotion holds the tension of the now and the not-yet as we march together to the agony of the cross and the jubilation of the resurrection."

TABITHA WESTBROOK, Author; Counselor

"I loved these Lent devotions. Elyse writes beautifully about our beautiful Saviour, and her words helped me see more of his humility, grace, and unspeakably great love for undeserving sinners. At times, I was moved to tears. She also helped me see myself more clearly, in a way that drove me back to my Lord with an increased awareness of my need and his mercy. What a wonderful gift!"

CAROLYN LACEY, Bible Teacher; Author, *Extraordinary Hospitality (for Ordinary People)* and *Say the Right Thing*

"This wonderful companion for the Lenten season will demand your attention, affection, contemplation, and hope. Elyse writes with warmth, humor, vulnerability, and faithfulness, and she tells the stories of Jesus' life with curiosity and passion."

RACHEL JOY WELCHER, Author; Poet

"Elyse Fitzpatrick combines faithful biblical reflection, compassion, and profound gospel clarity. With her characteristic warmth, she invites readers into the Lenten season as a fresh encounter with the crucified and risen Christ, who befriends sinners, bears shame, and gives himself fully for us. Deeply comforting and theologically rich."

JUSTIN S. HOLCOMB, Bishop, Episcopal Diocese of Central Florida; Author, *God with Us* and *Rid of My Disgrace*; Seminary Professor

"A beautiful invitation to encounter the Jesus who welcomes the weary, the wounded, and the wandering. With her signature blend of gospel depth and pastoral warmth, Elyse Fitzpatrick lifts our eyes from shame and striving to the Savior who calls us friends. These daily reflections are soaked in grace and grounded in Scripture—an encouraging companion for anyone who needs a reminder of his relentless kindness."

COLLEEN RAMSER, Speaker; Author; Podcaster; Trauma Therapist

"Holy days and seasons can become boring and bland. If you would like to change that this Lent, this is your book. *Friend of Sinners* captures the pathos, the tears, the laughter, and the reality of Lent. You will go on a journey that just might change your life."

STEVE BROWN, Author; Broadcaster

"Elyse helps us look at interactions Jesus has on his journey to the cross and draws our attention to the love and emotions Jesus has all along the way. Elyse asks us, 'Can you hear the Savior as he pleads for mercy for us all?' What a grace. I loved how this book helped me to again delight in all Jesus came to do for the world."

DR. PAMELA MACRAE, Professor of Ministry to Women, Moody Bible Institute

"Not only are these Lent devotions grounded in the beauty of the gospel; they are also clever, witty, and incredibly moving. I promise you won't put this book down without being changed. It's gospel-rich from start to finish—vintage Elyse Fitzpatrick."

J.D. GREEAR, Pastor, The Summit Church, Raleigh-Durham, NC; Author, *Everyday Revolutionary* and *Just Ask*

"I loved this book, which helped me slow down and reflect and meditate on what it really means for Jesus to be the friend of sinners—to be *my* friend. Elyse has a wonderful way of taking us by the hand and leading us beyond what is happening on the surface so that we can truly see and identify with the hearts of the real, ordinary people who encounter Jesus in the Gospels. I was deeply moved and humbled, and left marvelling afresh at both how incredibly costly and incredibly precious Jesus' love for needy sinners like me is."

ANDREA TREVENNA, Women's Minister, St Nicholas Church, Sevenoaks, Kent, UK

Friend of Sinners

LENT
DEVOTIONS
ON FOLLOWING
THE CRUCIFIED
KING

Elyse Fitzpatrick

Friend of Sinners

Published by:
The Good Book Company

thegoodbook.com | thegoodbook.co.uk
thegoodbook.com.au | thegoodbook.co.nz

Every book published by The Good Book Company has been written by a human author and edited by a human editor. While AI tools are sometimes used to assist with research and support certain processes, all content has been created by a human author and thoroughly checked by our editorial team to ensure it is biblically faithful and pastorally wise.

Cover design by Faceout Studio | Design and art direction by André Parker

ISBN: 9781802543667 | JOB-008368 | Printed in India

To all the women and men who have loved the One who dared to speak truth to power and who follow in his footsteps at the cost of their comfort, status, and even their own lives. Keep speaking, friends. He is with you.

Contents

Introduction

Christians are weird. I am allowed to say that because I am one, and have been for over 50 years. Think about it. Christians observe two major holy days. One celebrates the virgin birth of a King, whimpering amid the filth of a livestock pen. The other retells the story of dawn visitors to an empty grave, peering into a tomb meant to hold that King's silent, decomposing body. Weird? Absolutely. And, depending on your familiarity with those unpleasant smells, even disgusting. But… holy? How could a holy King associate himself with the refuse permeating a barn or a grave? And why would we celebrate it? Surely there are other moments in this King's life that would make more sense to remember?

Of course, the baby who was also a holy King was wrapped as cleanly as possible. Decades later, spices would have been placed in the death shroud to try to disguise his body's stench. Yet what we are looking at is not tidy or pleasant, let alone regal. Honestly, if we had not already been inoculated against the strangeness of Christianity's story, it would be difficult not to guffaw or turn away in disgust, or possibly even tremble in dread. The life at the center of Christianity begins and ends in shame, disgrace, and frankly, bad smells. Nothing neat or outwardly praiseworthy here: barn and grave, refuse and decomposition. Maybe all this earthiness is meant to reveal something to us. And we'll spend the next seven weeks thinking about what that something might be.

In the pages that follow, we will join up with a whole range of people, many of them just like us: ordinary laborers, worried parents, sick children, confused and careworn people. We'll meet political pawns, bitter revolutionaries, destitute widows, heartbroken mourners, the religious elite, and even the recently dead. We will meet those who have been with King Jesus from the earliest days of his public ministry and have heard a teaching that is unlike anything they had heard before (Luke 4:32), and others who appear fleetingly but are healed or changed by his touch or his word. Some will believe. Some will resist. Jesus will make both friends and enemies everywhere he goes.

Among those original believers, you will meet men and women who were blinded to his true identity by their personal desire to befriend a victorious King. They had mistaken expectations and so were ultimately heartbroken by his death. Even among his closest friends, few foresaw the tomb that was his destination, and none believed in the resurrection. The women who were some of his most loyal friends carried spices to do the awful work death demands because they expected to find their friend cold and decaying. But then, years later, many of those same friends walked with eyes wide open into their own martyrdom because they had learned that that tomb was not an ending; it was the door into eternal life and their best friend's presence.

We live at a time during which many people admit that they feel alone. Yes, loneliness is epidemic, and whether we blame screens or political polarization or the disintegration of the family unit, people feel unmoored from true friendships. Deaths of despair have skyrocketed. And while limiting screen time and making community a priority are definitely good steps to take, not even our best friends can relieve the deep isolation that we feel. We all need relationship with someone who really knows us and really loves us, and I'm contending that this person came to earth and walked to his death 2,000 years ago because he wants to befriend and assure you too. Yes, I know this story is ancient. For sure, it is weird. But I also know that millions of people, including myself, have found soul-satisfying friendship with him. He was accused by his opponents of being a friend of sinners (Luke 7:34), and his followers, through the millennia, have enjoyed experiencing the truth of that charge.

So, here's my invitation: let's spend the next 40+ days together seeking Jesus, the friend who laid down his life so that you could know you are loved and welcomed. Let's see what it means to call this crucified King our dear friend. Maybe you've heard and believed this story your whole life. Perhaps not. Maybe you are thinking it is time to glance at it again. Wherever your starting point, here, today, at the beginning of our journey, know this: you are welcomed in this company of those befriended by a crucified and risen King.

The Beginning of Lent

Ash Wednesday

Ashes to Ashes, Dust to Dust

"Teach us to number our days carefully so that we may develop wisdom in our hearts."
(Psalm 90:12)

Read James 4:13-16

The phrase "Ashes to ashes, dust to dust" is weird. The words feel anachronistic, as if they do not belong in our 21st-century Western world. Honestly, aside from Ash Wednesday, the only time I hear them is when I am watching a British crime drama and the vicar solemnly recites them at a graveside while the murderer lurks in the background.

Why would anyone think it would be a good idea to say them in any other context, including while they smudge ashes on my forehead?

Yet on this day in many churches, the remains of last year's Palm Sunday branches are smeared on skin in the form of a cross. The branches that were once waved while hosannas were sung have been burned to ash. Words are spoken that I need to hear, even though they are jarring: "Remember you are dust and to dust you shall return." Ashes to ashes. Dust to dust. Or this Latin phrase, *Memento mori:* remember your death.

All day, every day, I pretty much live as though I am not made of dust. Is it like that for you? Sure, I recognize that I am made of earthy elements like water, muscle, and bone, but though I admit to feeling my age now, I still assume I will just go on like this forever. Well, of course, maybe not forever, but for a good while longer. Surely it is not necessary to be so gloomy, is it? I mean, why would I need to remember my death? Why would you need to?

And while we are talking about those ashes, I confess to being concerned about how that cross will look on my forehead. Will it be pretty? Or will people think I failed to wash my face properly? Yes, even there in the recognition of my ultimate death, I remain concerned about my life, how I look. I do like appearing pious. I do not like looking dirty.

But that just underlines how much I need to hear it: *Elyse, remember your death.*

God's word says we are dust. However many technological breakthroughs the human race makes, however many medical advances we achieve, that will not change. We are not here forever. Life will end. To use another biblical metaphor, "You don't know the first thing about tomorrow. You're nothing but a wisp of fog, catching a brief bit of sun before disappearing" (James 4:14, MSG). A wisp of fog? Dust that blows away? Last year's ashes? That's me. And that feels weird to think about.

As we start our journey through Lent together, then, here is an encouragement: Remember who you are, and remember who he is. Remember that your life is short and that living in line with reality means living in a way that shows you are aware that you too are walking toward a tomb, just as the Lord Jesus did. If you forget—if you let your skewed expectations take up all the space in your heart—you will fail to see him, and you will struggle to grasp what he has done and is doing and will do for you. But when you forget, remember that he still sees you, and that he died for your forgetfulness.

In this devotional, we are on our way to a joyous celebration—Resurrection Sunday. But we are not there yet. First comes Ash Wednesday. It is only as you remember your death that you will learn to glory in his.

Reflect

How will you remember your death, and the death of Christ, today?

Thursday

Finding Him in the Wilderness

"And not only that, but we also boast in our afflictions, because we know that affliction produces endurance, endurance produces proven character, and proven character produces hope." (Romans 5:3-4)

Read Matthew 4:1-11

We are at the start of a seven-week journey to Easter. In these days of instantaneous everything, it may be a little daunting to commit to this. *Seven weeks?*[1] To get an idea of the length of this journey, scroll through your calendar to Easter Sunday. Does that seem like a long time? Of course seven weeks, or 40 days (without the Sundays), is not a *really* long time, but it is also not nothing.

And that not-nothingness is meant to remind you of something important. Lent lasts for 40 days for a reason.

These 40 days are meant to remind us of the time when…

---

1 Actually, it is a 7 week span of time and more than 40 days since Sundays are excluded.

Jesus was led by the Spirit into the wilderness to be tempted by the devil. After fasting forty days and forty nights, he was hungry. The tempter came to him… (Matthew 4:1-3, NIV)

It is not only our frenetic culture that needs Lent. The ancient church began this practice very early—it is first mentioned at the Council of Nicaea in 325 AD. Like us, they needed reminding that Jesus went 40 days without food or comfort, and that then, at the end of his time of starvation, isolation, and frailty, he fought temptation. Look again at your calendar and ask, "What would it be like to be completely cut off from all friends and food until Easter Sunday?"

Do not think that Jesus' deity meant he did not suffer like we would. He was "starving" (Matthew 4:2, CEB), but he did not access any super-powers to make his time of trial easier. He faced it as a flesh-and-blood human being. Sure, he had the Spirit's anointing and his Father's declaration of loving approval (Matthew 3:16-17), but still he suffered. And at the very end, when he was at his weakest physically, he fought intense temptation.

This wilderness trial strengthened Jesus' character. "Although he was the Son, he learned obedience from what he suffered" (Hebrews 5:8). Surely it was this experience he drew upon as he "determined to journey to Jerusalem" to die (Luke 9:51). He knew what was going to happen: "The Son of Man is about to be betrayed into the hands of men" (Luke 9:44). He was remembering his death: *memento mori*. He knew what he was about to face, and he drew on his habit of obedient suffering to steel himself to accept the Father's will.

Jesus' 40-day stay in the wilderness sets the length of our Lenten period. He sets us an example of resisting temptation by holding to the truth of God's word even when we are at our weakest, our tiredest, our loneliest (because isn't it when we feel these things that sin becomes so much more, well, tempting, and so much easier to excuse?). But those 40 days mean something more for us. Christ's victory over Satan, in the wilderness in weakness and then on the cross in ultimate weakness, is our victory too. Through faith in him, we already have his record of perfect obedience given to us—even when we fail to obey our Father, even when we forget him.

So, don't be afraid. Remember that even in the ways you fail, and even when you fail to remember, Jesus succeeded in your place. He is your leader and your example—he is also your Savior. It is with that freedom of knowing that our standing before God is secure in his victory that we can pray that these Lenten days will change us.

Reflect

How might setting apart the next 40 days teach you something about resisting temptation and the work of Christ?

Friday

Joining in His Suffering

"I am completing in my flesh what is lacking in Christ's afflictions for his body, that is, the church."
(Colossians 1:24)

Read Colossians 2:16-23

Much of the evangelical church today is allergic to any message of self-inflicted suffering such as what we might hear during Lent. Sometimes this is because people are rightly militating against a pietism that suggests that punishing ourselves will overcome sin or earn merit from God. No—the apostle Paul asserted that harsh treatment of the body has no value in "curbing self-indulgence" (Colossians 2:23). He knew that outward voluntary deprivation does not change our inward bent toward sin. In fact, it may worsen it through religious pride. I understand that allergic reaction against self-inflicted suffering. I feel it too.

And yet...

Personally, I did not observe Ash Wednesday until 2020, and I rarely gave the season of Lent much thought. But during the first year of the pandemic, my daughter invited me to go with her to an outdoor service. I was marked that day by more than ashes. I was reminded of what I had forgotten: voluntary suffering for the sake of Christ has significance. My voluntary suffering affects more than my individual life.

For years, I have focused my ministry upon the completed work of Jesus Christ and so have resisted any religious practices that might smack of merit-earning. Christianity is not a meritocracy. I believe that to the core of my being. "It is by grace you are saved, through faith—and this is not from yourselves, it is the gift of God—not by works, so that no one can boast" (Ephesians 2:8-9, NIV). How well you remember Lent, or how determined you are to fast in some way, will not, cannot, change God's disposition toward you in any way at all. If you trust him, you are already righteous in Christ, an infinitely beloved child of God, even if you put this book down and never get any farther on this Lenten journey. And fasting for Lent will not change your bent toward sin, nor will it earn anything from God.

So, why am I encouraging you to choose to fast?!

Let us consider Colossians 1:24, where Paul writes…

> *Now I rejoice in my sufferings for you, and I am completing in my flesh what is lacking in Christ's afflictions for his body, that is, the church.*

What is Paul talking about? If Jesus' life and death are already completely sufficient for our salvation (and they are), what made Paul say he needed to complete something that was lacking? Here is how I understand it: Jesus' afflictions have no deficiency when it comes to our salvation. But the church needed Paul's example, testimony, and work.

Today, as in Paul's day, a church needs its members to follow in the unlikely footsteps of their King and lay down their lives for others. Yes, it is true that God does not need our good deeds, but it is also true that our neighbor does. A willingness to suffer for others, to love our neighbors, has been the impulse of millions of Christians through millennia and should be ours today. Why were they able to do this? Because they were imitating their King. They were remembering their deaths and remembering his. Here's Paul again:

> *I am ready not only to be bound but also to die in Jerusalem for the name of the Lord Jesus. (Acts 21:13)*

A Lenten fast is a period of voluntary, small-scale suffering—a choice to go without, to teach yourself that Jesus is enough, and to prepare yourself to choose suffering for his people and his world rather than to run from it. Perhaps you could also use Lent as a period of service to your church or community in some particular way. Whatever way you choose to observe this season of Lent, I pray it will aid you in laying down this fleeting life in service of others, in service of his people, filling up Christ's afflictions for the sake of his body, the church.

Reflect

If you are thinking of choosing to fast, what could you go without in order to experience how Jesus is enough?

Saturday

The Glory Is Not Yet

"Wasn't it necessary for the Messiah to suffer these things and enter into his glory?" (Luke 24:26)

Read Luke 18:31-34

When Jesus foretold his death, the disciples thought the Lord was being needlessly pessimistic. They assumed that his successes meant the Romans would soon be overthrown and glory was close. So when he would say something like *I am on my way to die*, they simply could not hear it. I do not mean they were physically deaf. Rather, they were spiritually deaf. They could not hear his words because the story of "Humanity's Greatest Hits" was blaring on autoplay in their earbuds. They were consumed with thoughts like *Who gets to sit nearest your throne when we come into our... we mean **your**... kingdom?* The first time Jesus explained that he, the Messiah, had come to die, Peter even dared to try to set the Lord straight. "This will never happen to you!" *Don't be such a downer!* he chided (Matthew 16:22). In responding "Get behind me, Satan!" (v 23), Jesus sought to silence Peter's playlist. "You do not have in mind the concerns of God, but merely human concerns," he challenged him (NIV). But still Peter could not hear. The song was just too loud.

And Peter was not alone in his error.

After Jesus' death, two of his followers walked home from Jerusalem to Emmaus. All their plans for victory—"We were hoping that he was the one who was about to redeem Israel" (Luke 24:21)—had been crushed on a Roman cross. Yet it was not their hope for redemption that had been mistaken but their assumptions about what this redemption was and how it would happen. They had assumed there would be glory without suffering.

Not surprisingly, therefore, they failed to recognize the risen Jesus walking alongside them. All they could see was their ruined plans. Because they had stopped their ears whenever Jesus had said he was about to die, they had not heard what he had always said next—that he would rise again.

Jesus had always known that glory would come through and after suffering. So he asked them, "Wasn't it necessary for the Messiah to suffer these things and enter into his glory?" (Luke 24:26).

Necessary? Suffer? The juxtaposition of those two words troubles me. Everything in me screams that suffering cannot, should not, be "necessary." Sure, sometimes accidents happen, and plans often go awry. But *necessary*?

Jesus understood necessary suffering. He was "a man of suffering" (Isaiah 53:3). He learned its necessity throughout his life of deprivation and his 40-day fast followed by his battle with Satan. He learned it when his friends misunderstood his mission and clamored for power and position. He tasted it when he writhed in agony "on the night when he was betrayed" (1 Corinthians 11:23). He felt it when the crown of thorns was thrust upon his head and the lash tore open his back. And then… oh, my friends… he felt it when suffering tore him open to the depth of his soul at the loss of his Father's approving smile. And he cried, *Why?* (Matthew 27:46). Why indeed?

Underneath Jesus' tears was an understanding that the only thing that would reverse the curse and our complicity in it would be his suffering. Beneath Jesus' weeping eyes was a breaking heart of love, and of faith. He knew suffering was the first step toward his ultimate glory… and ours. He knew that after the suffering, his people would finally be able to see him and hear the truth. So it was that before he left them, those disciples in Emmaus had seen Jesus for who he is—the King who suffered and rose and now reigns in glory.

We want to jump ahead. We want to get past the suffering to the party. We want to sing "Christ the Lord is risen today! Hallelujah!" And that is not wrong. But we will not be able to understand his glorious message until our personal-ambition playlists have been silenced. And often they are silenced through suffering.[2] The Lenten season is a reminder that suffering comes before glory, and that in this life for us, as for our Lord, glory is secure but glory is not yet.

Reflect

What might choosing to go without teach you about suffering and glory?

2 Of course, this does not answer the whole "why?" question about suffering. But it was certainly the answer to the disciples' unbelief, shock, and discouragement at Jesus' crucifixion.

Sunday

A Sabbath Note

On Sundays you are encouraged to rest from your fast and rejoice in your King's grace, so there will not be any Sunday readings until Easter Sunday.

The First Week of Lent

His Shocking Arrival

Monday

Impossible Expectations

"When the time came to completion, God sent his Son, born of a woman..."
(Galatians 4:4)

Read Luke 1:24-25, 39-55

I know Lent is about Easter, not Christmas! But *memento mori* is part of the Christmas story too.

I am sure you remember the stories of the two unlikely women around whom the Christmas narrative is told: Elizabeth, the infertile, aged mother of John the Baptist and her younger relative Mary, the teenaged virgin who is the mother of Jesus. Both women conceived in impossible circumstances. Both women were honored in similarly strange ways. And both rejoiced at their exalted conditions.

When Elizabeth discovered she was pregnant, she "kept herself in seclusion for five months" (Luke 1:24), probably because she feared the shame she would feel if she miscarried. Once she reached her fifth month, though, she said, "The Lord has done this for me. He has looked with favor in these days to take away my disgrace among the people" (Luke 1:25). She had been called "childless" (v 36), but that identity would no longer define her.

When Elizabeth was six months along, the angel Gabriel visited Mary with a message of astonishing honor and promise—with the good news that every Jewish woman had longed to hear: "you have found favor with God" (Luke 1:30). Mary would give birth to the "Son of the Most High," who would be given the throne of David. "His kingdom will have no end" (v 32). Mary was the chosen one: the mother of the Messiah-King.

When Mary went to visit Elizabeth, both women broke out into joyful song. Elizabeth sang because she was filled with the Holy Spirit upon hearing Mary's greeting. Mary sang because Elizabeth's words emboldened her to give voice to her hopeful prophecy (v 46-55). Two unlikely mothers were rejoicing in each other's honor.

Elizabeth birthed John, and all we are told about his early life is that he "grew up and became strong in spirit, and he was in the wilderness until the day of his public appearance to Israel" (v 80). All was unremarkable aside from the fact that he eventually moved to the wilderness, where he would live rough—probably not the life Elizabeth might have envisioned for her only child. And then, after a period of public ministry and controversy, came his violent death—beheaded on the orders of King Herod and at the behest of his wife Herodias, for the crime of refusing to be silent about inconvenient truths (Mark 6:17-28).

Six months after John's birth, Mary gave birth to Jesus, the Messiah-King. After they returned home to Nazareth, Jesus, too, lived a normal life, on into adulthood. But for those 30 years, Mary surely turned over in her mind the words that Simeon had spoken to her about him days after his birth:

> *This child is destined to cause the fall and rise of many in Israel and to be a sign that will be opposed—and a sword will pierce your own soul. (Luke 2:34-35)*

Mary enjoyed the decades of relationship she had with her son, but after he left home and began public ministry, she seemed to lose the thread of his story (Mark 3:20-21). Had she forgotten the part about the sword? As she stood under the cross and watched a spear pierce Jesus' side, she surely did remember those words. *But I thought he would be a King... How is this possible?*

Both women had been chosen, called, and honored by God through the Holy Spirit's power. Yet both sons came to violent ends: John's head on a despot's dish, Jesus' body on a Roman cross. Both women knew joy and grief, life and death, smiles and tears. Mary witnessed the most miraculous of all births and the worst of all deaths... and learned that neither was the end of the story. She learned what it means to follow this Messiah.

So too for us. Being chosen, called, and honored by God will bring joy and life and smiles. But it will not insulate us from grief and death and tears. Remember death: but remember death is not the whole story. Enjoy lovely spring days of happiness and honor without forgetting death. And be comforted on darker days of difficulty and grief by remembering that death is not the end. Don't forget those ashes—or the resurrection to come.

Reflect

Life is full of both joy and sorrow, hope and despair. What are you experiencing now, and what difference is it making to know that both death and resurrection are to come?

Tuesday

The Lord Provides

"They don't have any wine."
(John 2:3)

Read John 2:1-12

I assume that by now you have decided whether and how you will fast. I do hope you will join me in a fast, but even if you decide not to, let me encourage you to keep on with your reading.

Jesus' first miracle feels like it has nothing to do with Lent. There's no fasting or suffering here. Our story is set at a party and seems to be all about solving a practical problem: the hosts have run out of wine. But on closer look, this is a story of one family's shame and Jesus' loving provision to cover them, and that's exactly what we need to hear during Lent.

The scene opens in the middle of the story with Jesus, his family, and disciples at an unnamed friend's wedding celebration. All we know about the hosts is that they failed to buy enough wine. It is hard, if we don't live in a shame-honor culture (and if we do enjoy convenient shopping options), to understand the gravity of their situation. In their context, the family might never recover from failing at proper hospitality on such an important occasion. As the wine ran low, a life of permanent, inescapable shame threatened to overtake them.

Jesus' mother knew the weight of public shame from her own season as a pregnant bride, and she knew the power of her firstborn son. So, she approached Jesus with the problem: "They don't have any wine" (John 2:3).

Jesus responded to her concern with what seems like a rude rebuff: "What has this concern of yours to do with me, woman? … My hour has not yet come" (v 4). It sounds as if he is saying, *That's not my problem, lady*—but he's not. Jesus knew that responding to this need would set off a series of events that would eventuate in his death, and so he challenged Mary to consider what she was asking of him. Yet still Mary understood Jesus' power and knew his generosity, so she told the servants to obey his directions (v 5). Mary knew the depth of Jesus' love for others, although perhaps she did not yet realize what his love would cost them both.

By commanding the servants to fill jars with ordinary water, Jesus set the stage for a miracle that would do more than supply the partygoers with something to drink—it would wash away their hosts' disgrace. But Jesus did even more than had been asked. He did not supply the celebration merely with enough mediocre wine. Rather, he flooded them with over 120 gallons of great wine—more than they could possibly need. Jesus both abundantly supplied good wine for his friends and lovingly protected his hosts' reputation. He willingly moved forward into the hour of his ministry that would end in his shame, his pain, his humiliation, and his death. All for the sake of us poor sinners, who can't even manage to throw a good party.

"Jesus did this, the first of his signs, in Cana of Galilee. He revealed his glory, and his disciples believed in him" (v 11). Jesus revealed his glory by covering over shame. He will not turn away from his people. His glory is still revealed as he covers our shame with his perfect, loving obedience. By his death and resurrection, he invites us into union with him. He is the Bridegroom, and the church is his bride, and his saving grace is the best wedding gift ever.

Maybe you are living in days of plenty and celebration: if so, rejoice deeply and without guilt, remembering that all you receive in this life is given by God and for his glory. But if you are living in days of humiliation, deprivation, or fear, remember that Jesus understands your weakness, knows intimately the pain of suffering, and covers your shame. You can ask him for grace to continue to believe. After Jesus' return and our resurrection, we will indeed drink delicious wine and eat soul-satisfying food… forever![3]

Reflect

What has Jesus given you that will you rejoice in and give thanks for today? What shame do you need Jesus to cover, that you can bring to him today?

---

3 See Isaiah 25:6.

Wednesday

Why Are You Asking Me for Water?

"I, the one speaking to you, am he."
(John 4:26)

Read John 4:7-30

Yesterday you read about wedding hosts who were facing humiliation and Jesus' miraculous gift to them of an honorable reputation. Today we encounter another story about thirst, water, and someone whose reputation had already suffered harm: the Samaritan woman.

Because it's easiest to understand the Bible according to our own context, we often miss the richness of Jesus' encounters with people. In this passage, Jesus led his followers to a town in Samaria and sat down at a well outside the town while his disciples went to buy food. As he waited, an unnamed Samaritan woman came to draw water. Typically, this story is told as though the Samaritan woman was immoral, based on the detail that she had had so many husbands (five) and was living with a man to whom she was not married. The proposed lesson is that Jesus graciously condescended to save even this scandalous woman.

As encouraging as that story might be, it overlooks how the woman might have ended up in that situation and misunderstands how Jesus might have viewed her. Let's redefine our understanding of the Samaritan woman. First, we should not assume that all her previous marriages ended in divorce. Because women frequently married older men, it would not be unusual at all for a woman to have been widowed at least once. Secondly, in those days women could not initiate divorce. If she had been divorced, we cannot assume it was her choice; and, sadly, it was common practice for men to trade wives in for newer models at their whim. Wives were often seen as nothing more than property. Finally, common-law arrangements were acceptable in certain circumstances and not that unusual.[4] A common-law living situation was certainly a more ideal situation than an unmarried woman's only other option: prostitution.

Unlike the wedding hosts who didn't procure enough wine, this woman had already lost her reputation, and not necessarily because of her own decisions or mistakes. She was also a Samaritan, a group of people that Jews usually despised. But not Jesus. He already knew and loved this woman, so he engaged her in a theological discussion about true worship before shockingly revealing himself to her as Messiah. In fact, she was the first non-Jew to hear this news from him, and she became the first evangelist to her people.

If Jesus had been interested in building a powerful empire, he would not have chosen her to be his emissary. He would have selected powerful men with trophy wives, plenty of sycophants, and Teflon reputations to be his representatives. Instead, weak and broken people would be his ambassadors.

The disciples did not understand. What would Jesus want

4 For instance, a Roman soldier might have decided to take her in as a permanent arrangement but by law could not marry her.

with a woman like that? But she didn't need their approval. She had met with Jesus and had been changed by him.

Jesus calls people who desperately need the living water that he is offering. His kingdom is full of sad women with too many husbands and questionable living arrangements, and full of clueless men who are shocked that Jesus would talk with someone like her (John 4:27). Why? Because Jesus' story is about his glory, not ours. When the Samaritan woman saw the glory of Jesus Christ before her, it changed her life. She was accepted by the King, and her shame was erased by her relationship with him. After encountering Jesus, she ran to tell all the people about him—people who, over the next few days, came to believe that he really was the Savior of the world (v 42).

Jesus was revealing the kind of King he is in what feels like all the wrong ways. Through suffering? Yes. Through outcasts? Yes. Through people just like us.

Reflect

Jesus welcomes all, even those with questionable resumés. How has your past led you to him, and how does that affect your gratitude to him?

Thursday

Gracious Forgiveness

"Since they could not pay it back, he graciously forgave them..."
(Luke 7:42)

Read Luke 7:1-17

As you read about Jesus' life, notice the worthiness of your Savior. He was not what the Jewish people expected him to be. He is so much more. He values people. Luke 7 recounts four very different people that Jesus met and valued: a Roman officer, a grieving widow, a "sinful woman," and an inhospitable Pharisee.

First, consider the benevolent centurion whose slave was gravely ill (Luke 7:2-10). Because this soldier had been so generous toward the Jewish people, the religious leaders asserted that he was worthy to receive Jesus' help. They were looking for a *quid pro quo*, and devaluing Jesus' generous compassion in the process. Despite their error, Jesus agreed to help. But while Jesus was on his way, the centurion sent word that Jesus need not trouble himself by coming to his house. As a true citizen of the empire, the centurion would have understood transactional relationships: *I scratch your back by doing charitable deeds; you reciprocate by healing my slave.*

But the centurion knew better—that he was not worthy, but could yet hope. And he was proved right when Jesus healed his servant.

Jesus doesn't offer miracles based upon what we can do for him. Instead Jesus extended his compassion to a man who could have been his enemy. Jesus likely knew that Rome would soon execute him, yet he helped this Roman soldier. *Are you tempted to think that your Lenten observance will make you worthy to receive Jesus' help?*

In the next encounter, Jesus happened upon a funeral procession and a widow whose only son had died (Luke 7:11-17). We are not told that this woman expressed faith or even asked for help. We hear of nothing that would deem her worthy to receive anything from the Lord. All we know is that "when the Lord saw her, he had compassion on her and said, 'Don't weep'" (Luke 7:13)—and raised her son to life. *How many times has Jesus graciously intervened in your life without your even asking?*

The third vignette is that of another unnamed woman with a bad reputation (Luke 7:36-50). Jesus had graciously accepted the invitation of Simon, a Pharisee, to dinner. While Jesus was reclining at the table, a "woman in the town who was a sinner" shockingly barged in and covered Jesus' feet with tears and kisses (v 37-38), and then dried them with her hair and lavished costly perfume on them. *And Jesus let her!* In fact, he welcomed her touch. She did not come to Jesus expecting anything. She knew there was nothing to commend her. Yet she was the only one in Luke 7 who seemed to fully grasp the worthiness of Jesus. So, she kissed him and wept and did the only thing she knew to do. *Do you believe that Jesus is not only worthy to receive your love but also welcomes your love, no matter what you have done?*

This third vignette is also about Simon, a self-righteous Pharisee who assumed he was already worthy. He considered

Jesus a fraud because Jesus let a sinful woman touch him. No true prophet would ever do that! Aware of Simon's thoughts, Jesus asked him this:

> *A creditor had two debtors. One owed five hundred denarii, and the other fifty. Since they could not pay it back, he graciously forgave them both. So, which of them will love him more? (v 41-42)*

Can you sense Simon's discomfort as he equivocated: "I *suppose* the one he forgave more" (v 43, emphasis added). Then Jesus dismantled Simon's self-righteousness by confronting him over breaking every rule of hospitality (no water, no kiss, and no anointing oil), but this woman, whom Simon had judged as sinful, had completed every step of hospitality in Simon's place. *Is there a type of person who, you assume, will not, or should not, be welcomed by Jesus? How might reflecting on how great a debt Jesus has forgiven you change your heart towards that person—and towards Jesus?*

Reflect

Which person in Luke 7 do you relate to? How does their story impact how you understand and appreciate the love of Jesus?

Friday

Audacious Faith

"Daughter ... Go in peace ..."
(Mark 5:34)

Read Mark 5:25-34

You might be most familiar with the desperate woman in today's reading as "the bleeding woman," but we're going to give her the dignity of the name she is known by in church tradition: Veronica. Veronica was not merely sick; she was afflicted (Mark 5:29) and had been for twelve years (v 25). The Greek word translated as "affliction" can also mean "beaten with a whip."[5] Veronica was afflicted, beaten down in every part of her life, and that made her desperate.

Veronica had bled for twelve years at a time when feminine hygiene products were nonexistent. If you are a woman, you have probably experienced some period shame: the embarrassment or shame experienced when feminine products fail to protect.[6] Veronica knew that feeling all

---

5 The Greek word is *mastix*, which "refers literally to a whip or flogging, metaphorically to affliction brought on by illness" (Chris Byrley, "Sickness and Disability," ed. Douglas Mangum et al., *Lexham Theological Wordbook*, Lexham Bible Reference Series (Lexham Press, 2014)).

6 For more on the topic see Rachel Jones, *A Brief Theology of Periods: Yes, Really* (The Good Book Company, 2024).

the time; and, to all this shame we can add that she likely suffered anemia, pain, and impoverishment. Her chronic uncleanness would have made her an outcast. She was afflicted in body and soul: financially, emotionally, socially, and religiously. She had received twelve years of blows, squandering all she had on useless treatments because the life she was living was a living death. She did not need to be told to remember her death—she was living it.

But then she heard about Jesus.

Veronica presumably "came up behind him in the crowd and touched his clothing" (v 27) because she thought her touch would defile Jesus and bring blows of censure down on her. So she looked for healing from a secret touch of his clothing. What beautiful audacity! Imagine surreptitiously sneaking up to take something from God!

Jesus immediately sensed the power that had gone out from him and wanted to know why. Yet he was not offended. He did not chide; he loved that she was healed.

Veronica expected to grab her healing and run. She had faith, but she was not bold enough to approach Jesus publicly. But Jesus would not allow her to slink back into the shadows. Although she would have settled for a healer, he would not settle for anything less than a daughter. Jesus forced her out of the shadow and into the light of relationship with him. He did not just offer healing but called her "Daughter": "Go in peace and be healed from your affliction" (v 34). Jesus' healing stopped the beating-downs and the suffering of her illness. He claimed her as his own daughter, welcoming her into his royal family.

He extends his Spirit's healing to you, too, offering his peace even to your most intimate self. This story reminds us of both *memento mori* and new life. If there are places in your body that you have hidden in shame, Jesus is there to heal and make you whole. Even if you don't experience physical healing yet, his death and resurrection free you from sin and from shame. If your suffering makes you feel like an outcast, remember: Jesus took all the beatings and bled out under his Father's censure so that you would be his. Go in peace, Daughter or Son of the King.

I doubt whether many of my readers would say they are free from affliction or shame, especially in their reproductive organs. Perhaps you are the source of the shame: maybe you have used your body in ungodly ways. Perhaps others are the source: maybe you have been used or abused and still bear those scars. Or perhaps your body just does not function as you had hoped it would. What shame still torments you? As you reach toward him, hear the Lord's voice to you today, gently calling you "Son" or "Daughter": *Go in peace and be healed from your shame.*

Reflect

Jesus loves the afflicted. What broken or shame-ridden places do you need to bring before him and ask for healing?

Saturday

Don't Be Afraid

"Don't be afraid; just believe."
(Mark 5:36, NIV)

Read Mark 5:21-24, 35-43

Today we meet another daughter, a dying little girl—the daughter of Jairus, a synagogue leader. When Jairus sought his daughter's healing, he approached Jesus in all the proper ways: he fell on his knees and begged Jesus earnestly to come and heal his daughter. Jesus gladly went with him—but while he was restoring health, respectability, life, and peace to Veronica, *memento mori* arrived in a message for Jairus: "Your daughter is dead. Why bother the teacher anymore?" (Mark 5:35).

Imagine how Jairus felt at that moment. In a brief time, he likely went from hope to desperation. Jairus had no idea what Jesus would do. He wasn't expecting that Jesus would raise his daughter from the dead. Hope for healing was one thing. The possibility of resurrection was unthinkable. Jairus might have been tormented by questions and doubts: *Why did Jesus stop along the way? Why did this brash woman have to choose this journey to interrupt? Why didn't God sustain my daughter until Jesus arrived?*

I have had many occasions when I have asked similar questions. I recall one particular time when my dear mother-in-law, Thelma, had fallen into a dementia that made her confused and fearful all the time. She was even becoming violent. I questioned why such a godly woman, who had spent her life in service of others and had led many to faith, was consigned to such darkness. Why was God allowing her brain to degenerate like this? Why did she have to spend her final days in fear? One day, I went on a walk. I was praying for her and listening to a sermon by Tim Keller on this very passage in Mark. In the sermon, he said something like, "If you knew what God knows and if you loved as God loves, you would understand."[7] I did not understand, but I did believe that God understood and loved. And I found peace.

Jesus offered a pathway to peace for Jairus as well: "Don't be afraid. Only believe" (v 36). When Jesus finally arrived at Jairus' home, he took the child by the hand and said these words: "Talitha koum … Little girl, I say to you, get up" (v 41). *And she did.* Her parents and Jesus' disciples were utterly astounded. Life from death? What is this? Better yet, *who* is this? The King over life and death? Yes.

Maybe there is an area in your life where you have experienced a whiplash of emotions like Jairus. Maybe it's the happiness you felt when you finally landed that job or your beloved said yes or the doctor's report finally read, "Cancer-free." Jairus had received Jesus' yes to come heal his daughter and believed that everything would finally be okay. But then the grave news came to him, as it comes to us: the job or the marriage or your body speaks *memento mori,* and everything turns to dust. So you ask, "Why me?" "Why this?" "Why now?" "Why a 'yes' that gave me hope and now a 'no'

7 Keller often made this point. See, for instance, goodreads.com/quotes/338379-god-will-only-give-you-what-you-would-have-asked. Accessed June 9, 2025.

that seems more crushing because of the hope I'd had?" I understand. But more importantly, so does Jesus.

Jesus' words to Jairus are his words to us today: "Don't be afraid. Only believe." Does that mean that all the sadnesses will now be wonderful? Will we all live happily ever after? No. It means that he sees, and he knows, and he holds it all in his hands. You are not alone. He will not forget your needs. He will not fail to act. Just believe.

Reflect

In what area of your life are you trying to fight fear and believe?

The Second Week of Lent

The Words of the King

Monday

An Invitation into Mercy

"I desire mercy and not sacrifice."
(Matthew 9:13)

Read Matthew 9:9-13

Did one of your parents ever warn, "You are known by the company you keep"? I am sure I told my kids the same thing. When my children were young, I taught them Proverbs 13:20: "The one who walks with the wise will become wise, but a companion of fools will suffer harm." Honestly, what I usually meant by that was "Don't hang out with that guy. I don't trust him." While that underlying message may have been wise counsel for my children, it was something our unlikely King ignored.

In his Gospel, Matthew honestly recounts his own story of meeting Jesus. Jesus "saw a man sitting at the tax office." (Matthew 9:9). At some point in his life, Matthew had decided to betray his Jewish identity and go to work for the Roman Empire. We don't know his motivation. We don't know if he became a tax collector because he loved money, valued the safety of Rome's approval, or was apathetic about his nationality. What we are told is that Jesus "saw him." Jesus was fully aware of everyone around him. There was no one he ignored; no one he would shun.

"Follow me," Jesus invited the tax collector. And Matthew, a man who had spent his life ensconced comfortably while oppressing his own people, responded. He "got up and followed him." Two words, "Follow me," prompted Matthew's transformation, freedom, and salvation. And then what did Matthew do? He threw a party.

> *While he was reclining at the table in the house, many tax collectors and sinners came to eat with Jesus and his disciples. When the Pharisees saw this, they asked his disciples, "Why does your teacher eat with tax collectors and sinners?" (v 10-11)*

Why did Jesus hang around with sinners? Because, according to the parable of the great banquet in Luke 14, Jesus knew that his Father had a party planned and that he wanted the banquet hall to be full (Luke 14:15-23). All his respectable invitees declined: "Without exception they all began to make excuses" (v 18). So he threw the doors open. In came "the poor, maimed, blind, and lame," who lived in the "streets and alleys of the city." You get the picture. Instead of closing the doors on the undesirables, Jesus flung them open. He knew that if only the truly righteous received an invitation, it would be a really small party. In fact, without his help, no one could come. So, he came to us to invite us in. He said, "Follow me" to Matthew, and he says it to us today, too.

Jesus befriended both the rich who inhabited tax offices and poor alley-dwellers. The gift of grace he had to offer them superseded cautions about unwise associations. No wonder the religious leaders hated him. When they accused him of being a "friend of … sinners" (Luke 7:34), it was no false taunt. They were not merely criticizing his taste in friends.

They were accusing him of being a sinner himself. Another time they even claimed that he was demon-possessed (John 8:52). They missed the whole point. Here was a friend of sinners who never sinned: a man who came to invite sinners in to perfection.

Jesus saw beyond outward appearances and knew his friendship could recreate a truly good person in place of the sinners he called. Jesus' actions overflowed from a heart filled with mercy. Like his Father, he prizes mercy, not sacrifice. He came from his Father not to call the righteous but sinners. (Matthew 9:13). So, he invited Matthew to follow him. He's inviting you, too, into a life of mercy received and mercy given.

During these Lenten days, he's calling us to be merciful, not merely religious. Being religious is easy. Following Jesus into a life of mercy is not. It demands that we extend mercy to all. Yes, even to *them*.

Reflect

What does it mean to you that the Friend of Sinners calls you his friend? How are you changed by his friendship?

Tuesday

Who can be Saved?

"With man this is impossible, but with God all things are possible." (Matthew 19:26)

Read Matthew 19:13-26

Jesus' disciples falsely assumed he needed protecting from the riffraff, whom they deemed unworthy of his notice. *Don't waste the Rabbi's time!* they may have muttered as they shooed parents away. *He's way too important to mess about with children.*

Jesus sternly replied, "Leave the little children alone, and don't try to keep them from coming to me, because the kingdom of heaven belongs to such as these" (Matthew 19:14).

"Just then" (v 16) another young person came to him, but this one was different. He had already accumulated status and wealth and a grand reputation. "I have kept" the law, he proudly assured Jesus (v 20). So why was he there? Maybe he wanted the proverbial pat on the back from the latest cool rabbi, or maybe he was a meticulous perfectionist who still felt insecure no matter how carefully he followed the rules. In any case, Jesus knew what made it hard for the young man to come to him.

The young man wanted assurance, but Jesus saw that what the young man really needed was to be free:

> *If you want to be perfect … go, sell your belongings and give to the poor, and you will have treasure in heaven. Then come, follow me. (v 21)*

You want to be perfect? Get insignificant. Get small. Become like a little child. See yourself as I see you: a beloved child whose insufficiencies are covered by perfection.

But alas, "when the young man heard that, he went away grieving, because he had many possessions" (v 21-22). The young man's many possessions, which seemed like a blessing, were actually crushing him. He could not rest because he was trying to drag his obedience and possessions into the kingdom. But his money did not mean God was pleased with him. In fact, it did not mean anything at all. It was not the blessing he thought it was. The door to life was wide open for him, but the way in was narrow (Matthew 7:14). He would need to shed all his worldly stuff and all his self-righteousness to enter. How could he do that? He could not. He would not. He walked away.

"Looking at him, Jesus loved him" (Mark 10:21). Oh my.

When the disciples heard that it was hard for the rich to get into the kingdom of heaven, they were utterly astounded and asked, "Then who can be saved?" (Matthew 19:25). Good question. The young, wealthy perfectionist and the status-loving disciples were equally confused. They both thought prestige, power, and cash were symbols of God's favor. They were wrong. And yet… looking at them all, the King loved them.

Jesus loved both the rich and the poor; he loved the sinner and the self-righteous. He loved them enough to lay his life down to become the door through which they could enter into eternal life (John 10:7). Whatever "camel … through the eye of a needle" in Matthew 19:24 means, it certainly represents that salvation by your own power is impossible. Jesus is the only door through which rich and powerful and little and weak "camels" must enter. The rich man could not save himself. But God could.

Why does the kingdom belong to little children? Maybe it's because they're too weak to try to place their trust in their own strength, or maybe it's because they haven't had time to accumulate a love of the things of this world yet.

And yet, Jesus loves and assures us all. Here's how we might imagine him comforting us: *What is impossible for you became possible because I emptied myself and was poured down into human flesh, and became a microscopic embryo for you. Fear not. My love is for all, even you. But you must come in naked and let me clothe you. I can do this for you because I had everything stripped from me on the cross so you could be dressed in beautiful robes of righteousness. And because I love you, "with God all things are possible"—yes, even my gift to you of friendship with me for eternal life.*

Reflect

Are you more like the little children or the rich young ruler? How is God transforming your faith in this season of Lent?

Wednesday

Forgiveness First

"Son, your sins are forgiven."
(Mark 2:5)

Read Mark 2:1-12

The story of the paralyzed man whose friends jumped the line to get him in front of Jesus is a familiar one. Well, okay, maybe they did not jump the line. No, they "dug through" a roof and dropped their friend onto Jesus' lap. Rude!

Recently I had to have roof and ceiling work done in my house. Sheets of vinyl were taped to the ceiling to seal off the debris, which was then carefully bagged up and thrown away. And still there was an immense mess. You can bet on the fact that Jesus was covered with whatever fell from above... Dust? Straw? Mud? Animal refuse? It got on his clothes and in his hair. Jesus' determination to befriend sinners meant that their messes would become his. He would not refuse to help just because he wanted to keep his hair, his clothes, his reputation clean. No, he knew what befriending the broken would mean, and he was willing to let their mess cover him.

Imagine how everyone around Jesus felt as that filth fell on them. They did not know that being near this most pure of all men would mean that they too would be covered with other peoples' messes. They learned that loving the desperate demanded a willingness to be pushed outside of their own tidiness into situations they would never choose for themselves. It is no different for Jesus' followers today.

Undoubtedly, of course, the paralyzed man and his friends were hoping for healing. What were the words he and his friends were hoping to hear? *Your body is healed.*

Instead, Jesus said, "Son, your sins are forgiven" (Mark 2:5).

For those of us reading this story now, it is easy to think, *Ah... what beautiful words!* And yes, they are beautiful. But they would not have been beautiful to this physically broken man and his friends. They would have been deeply disappointing and confusing. If they had not been so shocked, they might have responded with a *Thanks, but that's not why we're here. Can't you see he needs something more than spiritual blessings, as nice as that is? Can't you see how he's unable to do anything for himself?* And perhaps that is the point: Jesus willingly receives the mess that this crippled man brings and then gives him what he could never earn, even if he were completely able-bodied. This paralyzed man is not alone. No, we are all the spiritually disabled, who need to bring our weakness and mess to Jesus so that he can tell us that we are forgiven and welcomed there at his feet. *But what about my plans, my hopes, my prayers?* He knows. His answer may instead be *Not yet. But know that I see your faith, and you are loved and forgiven.*

I am sure you can guess how the religious elite responded. They did not like Jesus' use of words like *You are forgiven.* And so, to show them that he had divine authority to forgive sins, Jesus said to the man, "I tell you: get up, take your mat, and go home." And he did: "Immediately he got up, took the mat, and went out in front of everyone" (v 11-12). The reset of his life that he and his friends had desperately desired was his, but not until the reset of his soul had been achieved. Yes, Jesus healed this man. And sometimes, even often, he heals our bodies too. But at other times he does not, and it is then that we learn to lay patiently at his feet, resting in the love and forgiveness he so freely gives, knowing that our inabilities are covered by his righteousness.

Those standing around were "all astounded and gave glory to God, saying, 'We have never seen anything like this!'" (v 12). We have never seen nor even imagined a King who would gladly allow himself to be called the friend of sinners. They spoke it as an insult. He took it as his highest honor—even as people with their mess came to him, even as it eventually led him to the cross.

Reflect

"Your sins are forgiven." What does it mean to you to know that this is Jesus' word to anyone who comes to him in faith today?

Thursday

Just for Show

"This poor widow has put in more than all of them."
(Luke 21:3)

Read Luke 20:45 - 21:6

What are you proud of? What makes you feel like you have value?

We might get a clue about our true answers to those questions by looking at what we post on social media or how much we talk about the winning record of our favorite sports team. What do the pictures we post of our amazing desserts or vacations say about what we think gives us value? Sometimes we can answer that question by reading our online bios or remembering the humble brags we've snuck into casual conversation or prayer requests.

When my children were toddlers, I owned a Volvo station wagon that I was proud of. I remember parking near the entrance to their Tiny Tot class so that the other mothers there (to whom I felt inferior) would see that I drove a nice car. Ridiculous, right?

On a much less trivial note, for many years I placed my value in my religious accomplishments and being accepted in certain religious circles. That worked for a while… until it didn't.

Who knows how much of my ambition or accumulation of stuff (cars, houses, shoes, decor, my degrees, my kids' degrees, books, invitations to inner-circle events) I have poured my value-seeking desires into—how much has been, as Jesus said, "just for show" (Luke 20:45-47)? The trouble with my unending craving for significance is that I can never do enough to fill the bottomless abyss of my terrifyingly needy ego.

Religious people in ancient times did the same thing. Jesus said that they loved their long robes, greetings in the marketplace, best seats in the synagogue, and places of honor at banquets. The rich loved to hear the sound of their coins echoing in the temple treasury and their own voices raised in long prayers, just for show. Later in history, churches were adorned with beautiful stones and gifts dedicated to God, accompanied by plaques naming the donors (just for showing gratitude, of course…). Same story, different millennium.

It's tempting to think that all this glory-chasing is victimless. But Jesus understood the effect that glory-chasing had on the vulnerable. He said that the proud "devour widows' houses" (v 47). The backs of the poor and socially insignificant have always been convenient stepping-stones to increased power, status, and reputation for "the great."

Jesus noticed others because he was not focused on himself. He was not seeking his own glory and did nothing just for show (John 8:50). So, among all the people striving for the worship of others, he noticed an impoverished widow dropping in "two small copper coins" which was "all she had to live on" (Luke 21:2, 4, ESV). The days of lovely clothes and respectful greetings at dinner parties were long over (if they had ever existed) for this destitute woman. Perhaps this was the last act of her life; we do not know. But we do know that she had Jesus' attention. He saw her, loved her, and spoke words of approval over her. While the disciples and religious leaders were busy being impressed by and concerned with their standing among their peers and their impressive buildings, Jesus saw what mattered to his Father and praised it: the quiet, dependent, truly generous faith of the humble.

Jesus noticed people, but he also noticed the time. He knew that soon the curtain would fall on the Jewish leaders' showy, outward acts of religion. About 40 years later, the Romans would sack their city and destroy their temple. He warned, "The days will come when not one stone will be left on another" (v 6). All their proud parading would be shown for what it was: dusty rubble.

Living with *memento mori* in mind includes humbly facing the reality of our transient lives. We are dust, and all our posturing and glory-seeking will return to dust. Our lives, all we have, belong to the King, the one who sees and loves us. Yes, he sees, loves, and is pleased with us.

Reflect

What would look different in your life if you sought only the glory that comes from God and not the approval of others?

Friday

Wildflowers... Just Because

"Don't be afraid, little flock, because your Father delights to give you the kingdom." (Luke 12:32)

Read Luke 12:22-34

Although I have spoken and written about worry extensively, I still find myself struggling with it often. Because I tend toward pessimism, it is hard for me to assume that things will work out nicely. My dear husband, Phil, recognizes that he is a "The Sun Will Come Out Tomorrow" kind of guy, while diagnosing me as a "Paint It Black" sort of person.[8] He's right. And I am sure his interior life is far more pleasant than mine. Some days I have to struggle to believe that there even is a sun, whether it may come out tomorrow or not.

I desperately need to hear the King's counsel about worry. He reminds me that life is more than food and the body is more than clothing. The outward trappings of the life I want are not the true substance of what matters.

---

8 The song "The Sun Will Come Out Tomorrow" is from the Broadway musical Annie, written by composer Charles Strouse and lyricist Martin Charnin. "Paint It, Black" is by The Rolling Stones, written by Mick Jagger and Keith Richards.

The original hearers of Jesus' words often subsisted from day to day with only one or two pieces of clothing and no side-by-side refrigerators packed with food. Their concerns and worries were far more grounded in actual desperation than ours. And yet worry is a still a common pitfall for us today. Apparently, gaining possessions, whether a few or a lot, is not the antidote to worry.

Jesus invites us to look up and away from our need, to see the beauty he creates. *Look at the birds. Consider the wildflowers.* My incessant inward focus blinds me to the beauty all around me: creatures that our Creator is mindful of and sustaining without my notice, worry, or help; wildflowers he causes to grow just because. I once saw a field of wildflowers growing on a deserted plain deep in Mexico. As far as I could tell, these flowers were not there because anyone tended them or even saw them. They grew because God loves beauty. They blossomed just because God cared for them.

The season of Lent helps us get our vision focused outward. Take some time today to see the King's creation. Then meditate on this: *you are of more value to him than all the glorious universe he has made.* Every wonderful bird exists under his care. He feeds them and knows when they fall to the ground. Yet you are of more value than they. That magnificent carpet of wildflowers or even the little daffodil cautiously poking her head up now, hoping the snows are over, is more beautiful than all the treasures packed into your fridge and closets and life. Yet tomorrow it will all be "thrown into the furnace" (Luke 12:28). All of creation is under the watchful eye of the King. He "clothes" the fields for our mutual pleasure. Yes, he delights in it, but he delights in us even more.

Jesus calls us to a sabbath rest where we can stop striving to accumulate. Look at what he has already done. Consider the birds and the lilies. Take in a restful breath or two. (Really, do it now.) Now experience the rest of knowing you have a Father who values you (v 24, 30). He is no deadbeat dad. He sees you, knows you, and values you because you are his creation and beloved child. And he thinks you are beautiful. Yes, you.

This amazing truth allows us to stop striving, stop building bigger barns, and become radically generous people, depositing into an "inexhaustible treasure" in heaven (v 33). Remembering how we are welcomed, loved, and provided for enables us to seek his kingdom, not our own. It frees our hands to receive the magnificent life he delights to bestow. And if we *memento mori*, we will see that God holds both our life and death in his loving hands. "Don't be afraid, little flock, because your Father delights to give you the kingdom" (v 32).

Reflect

If you are able, go outside today. Notice God's care of creation and let it remind you about his care for you. Take in a few deep breaths. Don't be afraid.

Saturday

Dying to Live

"For whoever wants to save his life will lose it, but whoever loses his life because of me will find it."
(Matthew 16:25)

Read Matthew 16:21-28

Recently I was interviewed about my involvement with asylum seekers at the California/Mexico border. The reporter did not have any religious background but was trying to understand why many evangelicals hold distinctly different perspectives from each other about immigration. Weren't we all following the same Jesus? I told him that I cared about the vulnerable at the border because Jesus saw and cared about me when I was like them: looking in from the broken outside. So, I knew I had to do the same. I told him about the King's heart to lay down his life for others. Then I invited the reporter to lose his life so he could find it in Jesus.

I fear the church has done a pretty crummy job of discipling her members to fulfill the true call of Jesus. Jesus doesn't call us to follow him so that we can be financially blessed or popular, or experience comfort and ease. That kind of call would not have prepared early Christians to expect that they might become entertaining dinner entrées for lions in the Coliseum. Rome would not have persecuted this new religious movement if it had followed the life of hedonism and comfort that Rome promoted. That kind of Jesus could easily have been incorporated into Rome's pantheon of other gods, because there would have been no call for any sort of radical allegiance to a different king and no call to lay down one's life. Choosing to lose everything to find real life was part of what made Christians anathema to Rome. Rome was for winners, the powerful, the in-charge. Certainly not for slaves or foreigners on their way to the arena.

Right after proclaiming the ultimate victory of his church (Matthew 16:18), the King foretold his upcoming death. He said that it was necessary for him to suffer many things, to go to Jerusalem, and to be killed. Peter rebuked him: "Oh no, Lord. This will never happen to you!" (v 22). Jesus responded to Peter's misguided efforts to protect him by calling him the devil and telling him that he had his priorities all wrong. Jesus said Peter was a hindrance, a trap—not a loyal friend. Instead of thanking Peter for trying to protect him, Jesus upped the ante:

> *If anyone wants to follow after me, let him deny himself, take up his cross, and follow me. For whoever wants to save his life will lose it, but whoever loses his life because of me will find it. (v 24-25)*

In other words, the call to follow King Jesus is a call to come and die. It's a call to say "no" to every siren's seductive song that whispers that real happiness is found in the pursuit of ease and power, especially power over the vulnerable. It is a call to follow him into the places avoided by the respectable people and join him in his walk up the hill toward Golgotha and the door to true life.

This is the choice Peter faced. It is the choice we face as well: either you put aside your desire for power, fame, and ease to pick up your cross and follow your humble Savior, or you choose to lose your life to the futile idols of this world. You cannot have both. None of us can.

Think again about Jesus' somber words: "For whoever wants to save his life will lose it, but whoever loses his life because of me will find it." This call asks us to *memento mori*. Death is coming. You will lose your life—we all do. No one gets out of here alive. The choice is about how you lose it. You can lose your life while vainly striving to save it, or you can lose it now by giving it away in service to him and others, and in doing so find eternal life. His invitation stands: come and die so that you might live.

Reflect

How do people usually explain what it looks like to follow Jesus? In what parts of your life are you being called to deny yourself and take up your cross?

The Third Week of Lent

An Upside-Down Kingdom

Monday

What Makes Angels Dance?

"I tell you, in the same way, there will be more joy in heaven over one sinner who repents than over ninety-nine righteous people who don't need repentance ."
(Luke 15:7)

Read Luke 14:33 – 15:7

Again and again, Jesus welcomed the riffraff and confronted the religious elite. In Luke's narrative, Jesus taught the cost of discipleship: *Hate your family! Take up your cross!* (Luke 14:25-27). He urged them to seriously consider the cost of following him. It is not a stroll in the park. It means that you must "renounce all [your] possessions" (v 33). If you do this, you will be like salt, distinctive from others yet flavor-enhancing, preserving the living in a decaying culture enamored by wealth and power. If you are unwilling to do that, you have become worthless to the kingdom. You are fit only for the manure pile (v 35). (Jesus' words, not mine.) As I have said before, the love of our possessions is a great hindrance to walking with the one who had "no place to lay his head" (Matthew 8:20).

Luke further portrays the two groups of people around Jesus: those who listened and those who judged. The ones who listened were the traitors and the sinners, sex workers, rule-breakers, foreigners, alley-dwellers, the outcasts. Life had taught them to keep their mouths shut; their silence enabled them to hear. Jesus' words spoke deeply to them. The ones whose mouths were full of judgmental words and complaints were the self-righteous religious elite. They were convinced that their opinions really mattered and would only attend dinner parties if the right sorts of people would be there.

Jesus sees the hearts of both kinds of people and tells them a story. Let me paraphrase:

> *Imagine you own 100 sheep and one wanders away. Being the great shepherds you are (cue snickering in the crowd), you'll surely leave the 99 rule-observing homebodies and go searching for that lost one. Right? (More snickering.) And, being wonderful shepherds who really love lost sheep, you would pick that rascally wanderer up and joyfully (yes, joyfully) carry it home on your shoulders. Talking to it, laughing with it. You would love having it there with you. Stupid, smelly sheep. Joyful shepherd. Then, when you get home, you don't scold that sheep or put it in a pen with other naughty fence-hoppers. No, you call your neighbors and throw a rowdy party. Right? (Cue stunned silence.)*

And then, just in case they failed to get the message, Jesus declared:

> *I tell you, in the same way, there will be more joy in heaven over one sinner who repents than over ninety-nine righteous people who don't need repentance. (Luke 15:7)*

Mic drop. Jesus explained that the people who cause joy in heaven are not the self-righteous ones, those who think they do not need to repent or change because they have already earned God's smile. Not at all. Rather, heaven overflows with gladness when sinners turn toward God and relax on his shoulders so he can happily bear them home. Heaven's party happens when a person sees their need, turns toward Jesus, and listens to his voice. Those are the people who make God laugh and the angels dance.

Do not misunderstand. Jesus is not saying that there are people who have no need of repentance. What he is saying is that there are people who know they are sinners and people who do not. The sinners who have learned that they just do not make the grade are shocked when they receive an invitation to the King's party. They are the ones who bring heaven cheer when they RSVP, "Wouldn't miss it for the world!"

On the other hand, it is the self-righteous and proud people who will find the door barred. They assume they walk under the countenance of God's smile. They are wrong. But even they would be welcome to come if they would be willing to let the Good Shepherd pick them up, carry them home, and seat them next to that formerly smelly rabble to enjoy a sumptuous dinner.

No matter how you see yourself, hear Jesus' invitation. Fill out that RSVP now. Heaven is waiting.

Reflect

Which category of people do you identify with? Are there impediments that you feel are preventing your entry into the party? Do they need to?

Tuesday

Old Wine Is Better

"For the Son of Man is Lord of the Sabbath."
(Matthew 12:8)

Read Luke 5:33-39; 6:1-11

As a woman in her 70s, I am not a huge fan of change. My life is like a comfy old pair of jeans: it fits effortlessly. Change is painful—especially for the "elderly," as my (former) doctor once called me.

Today you read how Jesus answered a Pharisee's question about fasting with a proclamation that he is the Bridegroom to be celebrated. At the end of the discussion, he told a parable about old wineskins and torn clothing: pouring new wine into old containers or sewing new fabric onto old cloth ruins them both. In the same way, trying to combine status quo religion with new-kingdom realities always fails. The new kingdom could not be merged with the old. Jesus was making the status-quo religious practices obsolete. Word of wisdom: never challenge a religious leader's status quo. You may get killed for it.

Aside from Jesus' poor choice of friends, nothing enraged his detractors more than his seeming disregard for the Sabbath. Of course, they would object that Sabbath observance was commanded in the law (Exodus 20:8-11), and they would be right. But the one who was the physical embodiment of God's law knew the true meaning of Sabbath rest. It was not about counting steps and making sure others did too; it was about resting in God's mercy for the hungry and hurting, and restoring flourishing to broken lives.

On seven occasions Jesus opposed the status quo by healing the hurting on the Sabbath:

- in a synagogue with a man whose hand was shriveled (Matthew 12:9-14)
- in Peter's home with his fevered mother-in-law (Mark 1:30)
- at home with a paralyzed young man (Mark 2:1-8)
- in a synagogue with a disabled woman (Luke 13:10-16)
- at a Pharisee's dinner party with a diseased man (Luke 14:1-6)
- a paralyzed man at the pool of Bethesda (John 5:1-16)
- a man born blind sitting outside the temple (John 9)

Seven times Jesus healed on the Sabbath, but instead of being grateful or rejoicing that people had been freed from illness, disability, poverty, or shame, the Pharisees (the self-appointed Sabbath police) were enraged. Who did he think he was?

Jesus understood that pride and self-righteousness drove their rule-keeping, not love for their neighbors, God's law, or even God himself. They had missed the point: Sabbath-keeping was about remembering the astounding gift of God in creation. He had graciously provided so that humanity could both flourish and rest. Paradoxically, they employed God's command to rest as an opportunity to work for their own righteousness. If they had let him, Jesus would have freed them too. He wanted to untie them and lead them to refreshment and safety , but they wouldn't have it. They were too busy policing "the riffraff."

Jesus protested, "The Sabbath was made for man and not man for the Sabbath" (Mark 2:27). Isn't it just like us to take a gift meant to be a refreshing drink and turn it into a deadly sludge? What had been meant as a joy-producing gift became a soul-crushing burden. Then the leaders employed it as a cudgel with which to beat others, including the Bridegroom and Lord of the Sabbath himself. But Jesus razed their status quo by loving his suffering neighbors, knowing all along where that would lead: yes, to Golgotha, but also to a tomb where all our vain labors might be abandoned.

The Bridegroom, the Lord of the Sabbath, is still pouring out goblets of delicious mercy. He invites you to drink up and rest. Sure, the drink might make you forget your conscience-assuaging traditions, but the freedom will be worth it. Of course, you might choose to be the person who, after drinking old wine for so long, refuses to try the new, "because he says, 'The old is better'" (Luke 5:39). It's not. Your loving Bridegroom knows… so drink up.

Reflect

On your next Sabbath, how will you remember the lavish generosity of the wine-pouring Bridegroom, the Lord of the Sabbath?

Wednesday

A Good Friend

"Lord, the one you love is sick."
(John 11:3)

Read John 11:1-44

Friendship implies obligation. When your friend texts, "I need help!" you drop everything and respond. Jesus' love for his friends is on full display in the well-known story of the raising of Lazarus from the dead (John 11:1-44).

It is tempting to read this story like a Sunday School lesson: Lazarus is sick. The sisters ask for help. Jesus ignores them. Lazarus dies. The sisters do not understand. Jesus raises Lazarus. Everyone lives happily ever after. The End. But the truth is so much deeper than this.

When Lazarus' sisters, Mary and Martha, sent word to Jesus, "Lord, the one you love is sick," they were likely expecting an immediate reaction. If Jesus found out that his friend was ill, he would surely drop everything to help him. But the Bible tells us that when Jesus received their message, he did not respond for two days.

Two days.

How are we supposed to think about that? What is the point of having friends in high places if help does not come when requested? How do we handle heaven's silence? How do the people around us try to make sense of God's silence in the midst of our suffering? Or, more pointedly, how do *you* handle heaven's silence? Sometimes we question if we must have some secret sin we need to repent of or insist that God is teaching us some lesson we were too dull to learn in less painful ways. As in Lazarus' case, these answers, reasonable as they may seem, just do not fit the reality of many of our stories.

When Mary and Martha sent the message to Jesus, they called Lazarus "the one you love." They did not point out any virtuous deeds Lazarus had done. Instead, they reminded Jesus of his love for his friend. They were hoping that love would move him to action. And yet, it feels like not even love was enough. Jesus did not budge. So eventually the sisters would whisper words like *The one you love is dead* and, likely, *Why?* through tears. Can you imagine the darkness that engulfed them—not just at the loss of their beloved brother but also at the failure of their friend (the Messiah, for crying out loud) to help them? *We thought he loved us. We thought he was powerful. We thought he would come.*

Have you ever prayed, "Where are you, Lord? Why aren't you here?" I have. Loads of times. I think, *Lord, here I am, trying to serve you, and you check out? I am heartbroken and devastated, and I can barely breathe. Why didn't you stop this from happening?* Even worse, if God's ways are so mysterious that we are blind to his plans, how are we supposed to live? If our suffering does not make sense, even when we try to think about it biblically, what are we supposed to do?

Yes, Jesus used the death of his friend to glorify himself (v 4), but none of us (and I mean none) would have seen a resurrection coming. Why not? Because our perception, our imagination, even our faith is broken. Yes, we are broken—but we are also dearly loved. And that, my friends, is our only hope. The one who died, rose, and ascended loves us. When we hurt, he weeps with us. We can, and should, bring him all our questions, but the answers may not be clear. What will always be true is that no matter what is happening in our lives, he is our loving Friend right now. He loves you right now. Maybe someday we will have answers, but in the meantime, we hold on to this one certainty: we are loved.

Reflect

A day is coming when the ones Jesus loves will no longer suffer. How does this encourage you today? Is there anyone else the Lord is nudging you to share this truth with?

Thursday

Envy's Fruit

"It is to your advantage that one man should die for the people rather than the whole nation perish." (John 11:50)

Read John 11:38-53

The resurrection of Lazarus was the final straw for the religious leaders. One event after another had piled up until the religious leaders felt they had to act. Sure, all of Jesus' consorting with sinners and healings on the Sabbath were troubling. And the way that he had addressed them in front of the crowds was humiliating. But when Jesus raised Lazarus from the dead, the die was cast. Jesus' execution was now not a matter of "if" but "when":

> *What are we going to do since this man is doing many signs? If we let him go on like this, everyone will believe in him, and the Romans will come and take away both our place and our nation. (John 11:47-48)*

Why did Jesus irritate them so? What were they afraid of? They feared that "everyone [would] believe in him" and that they would lose their power. They were afraid that Jesus might upset the precarious equilibrium they had created and the Romans would step in and impose even more severe governmental controls on them. Although they hated Roman rule, they liked their comfort even more. They loved their places of honor. Never underestimate the motivating power of comfort with the status quo and the fear-producing envy of others who might upset it. Jesus had to die. In their blindness, they could not see that Jesus would never want their kind of power. He had refused it before. He knew where it originated and what it did to a soul that welcomed it.

Not much later, these religious leaders would accuse Jesus and expect Pilate to sentence Jesus to death for them. But Pilate would see through their accusations. He would know that "it was because of envy that they had handed him over" (Matthew 27:18). Although Pilate was ambitious to his core, even he would clearly see what was happening. They did not care about lawbreaking or upholding governmental rule. They cared about their power and the possible loss of it.

Finally, Caiaphas the high priest put a stop to their grumbling:

> *You know nothing at all! You're not considering that it is to your advantage that one man should die for the people rather than the whole nation perish. (John 11:49-50)*

But Caiaphas knew "nothing at all" as well. He did not know that in speaking these words of Jesus' execution, he was in fact being moved by the Holy Spirit to prophesy about Jesus' mission in the world:

> *He did not say this on his own, but being high priest that year he prophesied that Jesus was going to die for the nation, and not for the nation only, but also to unite the scattered children of God. (v 51-52)*

Astounding words.

Yes, Jesus would die for the nation but also to "unite the scattered children of God." Finally, God would fulfill the words spoken to Abraham about the worldwide blessing of the promised one. And he would use the Pharisees' hunger for power and control to accomplish our salvation.

The psalmist had written prophetically about these events: that the rulers of the earth would "conspire together against the LORD and his Anointed One" (Psalm 2:2). God's response? He laughs (v 4). Nothing—neither the rulers of this world nor the devilish powers that motivate them—can stop God's plans. Nothing can overcome his love for his children. The religious leaders thought they could stop people from believing in Jesus. But here we are, thousands of years later: believers from every tribe, language, and nation, united in one kingdom because of the power of his resurrection.

Reflect

How could the worship of Jesus as your King free you from the envy of others' power and place?

Friday

Betting It All

"The house was filled with the fragrance of the perfume."
(John 12:3)

Read John 12:1-7

When Mary and Martha received their brother, Lazarus, back from death, Jesus turned their hopeless mourning into astonished joy. Six days before Jesus' impending death, Mary, Martha, and Lazarus hosted a dinner for their friend and his followers.

As usual, Martha was busy serving the gathered guests. Also as expected, Lazarus was "reclining at the table" with Jesus. But then the unexpected occurred: Mary took a pound of "pure and expensive" perfume, knelt before Jesus, and poured it out upon his feet and "wiped his feet with her hair" (John 12:3).

And Jesus let her.

It is easy for us to underestimate the impropriety of this action. A woman's covered hair was a sign of her modesty. Modest women never uncovered their hair, let alone let it fall before anyone other than their husband. And yet, here is Mary kneeling before her Messiah, caressing his feet and soothing them with fragrant oil.

And Jesus let her.

Jesus understood what she was doing. She was not touching him in a sexual manner, and he did not assume that by dint of her gender her actions were suspect. She was anointing his body before his execution. It was not that long ago that she had anointed her brother's dead body for burial. And here she was again, doing the same thing. But this time she was looking to the future. She had been listening to Jesus' words. His death was coming, and she acted as a faithful Israelite woman and prepared for the death of her beloved.

"So the house was filled with the fragrance of the perfume." Not long before, a tomb had been filled with the nauseating stench of her brother's decaying body. A massive stone had been rolled over the mouth of the tomb to entrap that horrible smell, a smell that proclaimed the death of his future and hope. Darkness, hopelessness, and death had filled this house. But now, Lazarus' home was filled with a fragrant aroma and the invaluable beauty of a loving, worshiping heart.

No one knows for sure where Mary got that expensive anointing oil. Perhaps it had been gifted to her as a dowry for a hoped-for betrothal. If that was the case, she had just given away her chances of marriage. She was betting it all. She was laying it all down: her future husband, her propriety, her reputation. Everything was gone now, except for her love for the rabbi who welcomed and enthralled her: the one who would eventually become her spiritual beloved Husband. Forsaking all others, and all she had, she was cleaving to him.

And he welcomed it.

Mary likely knew that Jesus' death was coming, but she could not foresee the resurrection. We are walking through days that will lead toward a death that Mary foresaw but also to a resurrection she was blind to. Yet even in her blindness, she bet it all. We know that resurrection was coming, so it is easy for us to just skip ahead—to rush by all the death and get to all the good smells. We want the happiness of Easter Sunday without the preceding days of confusion, loss, shockingly rash devotion and worship that would make it truly joyful. That's why these *memento mori* days are so good for us. Mary's example invites us to bet it all. Like Mary, will you kneel before the King and lay down your life in worship, no matter the cost?

Reflect

If you are able, kneel—really kneel—in prayer and worship like our sister Mary did, asking that the Lord would fill your heart with love and worship. In what other ways could you physically demonstrate wholehearted worship of your Savior today?

Saturday

Follow the Money

"Why wasn't this perfume sold …
and given to the poor?"
(John 12:5)

Read Psalm 49

Whenever my husband Phil and I are discussing why some person or entity took a certain action, we often quip, "Follow the money." Never underestimate the power of the love of money. Aside from surface trappings like access and comfort, money puts us in charge and creates the illusion that we are secure, sovereign, and omnipotent. "If wealth increases," the psalmist wrote, "don't set your heart on it" (Psalm 62:10). Why not? Because money is a dangerous deceiver. But while we may wholeheartedly agree with that sentiment, our lives often don't demonstrate that belief.

When Jesus said that we cannot serve both God and cash (Matthew 6:24), he wasn't suggesting that it would be nice if we helped the poor a little. He was making a statement of fact: it is impossible to have a heart determined to accumulate wealth *and* be his follower because you cannot serve two masters. Jesus' life was the antithesis of the Elon, Jeff, and Bill power structures of this age.

At least one of his disciples, Judas, just didn't get it.

On the heels of Mary's extravagant worship, Judas criticized her actions:

> *Then one of his disciples, Judas Iscariot (who was about to betray him), said, "Why wasn't this perfume sold for three hundred denarii and given to the poor?" He didn't say this because he cared about the poor but because he was a thief. He was in charge of the money-bag and would steal part of what was put in it. (John 12:4-6)*

Evidently, Judas thought he could love his rabbi and denarii and pretend he cared about the poor. But he was desperately wrong and heartbreakingly deceived. The love of money will do that to you. It will make you think that you are clever, that God wants you to be rich, and that you deserve it. It will talk you into betraying the one who loves you best. It will blind you to God's plan to bring salvation to the world through weakness. The one who had "no place to lay his head" (Matthew 8:20) was the one who knew what it would take to save the self-deceived money-grubbers of the world. Despite the power it affords, money could never save them. Judas fell into "temptation, a trap, and many foolish and harmful desires, which plunge people into ruin and destruction" (1 Timothy 6:9). It was, indeed, impossible for him to serve Jesus and money.

Judas had no qualms in criticizing Mary. His love of money and power apparently went hand in hand with a misogynistic view of "emotional women who did not know their place." His heart was so far from his rabbi's. So Jesus rebuked him: "Leave her alone!"—and maybe that's what sent him over the edge.

Judas rapidly plunged into ruin and destruction. "What are you willing to give me if I hand him over to you?" he asked the religious leaders (Matthew 26:14). *Thirty pieces of silver?*

Done. If I can't sell the perfume, then I'll sell my rabbi. And I'll do it with a kiss. "Greetings, Rabbi!" Judas would proclaim when his kiss betrayed Jesus (v 49).

Money promises blessing, but it ends up being a woeful curse. What happened to those precious pieces of silver after Jesus' arrest and sentencing? Judas threw them onto the floor of the temple, and because they were blood money, they were used to buy a plot of land to bury the poor. Ah, alas. Now on his way to kill himself, Judas would finally help the poor. He sought wealth. He gained death.

We should not be surprised by the actions of a Judas. We see them all around us, perhaps even in our own hearts. What should surprise us was Jesus still called Judas "Friend" (v 50). He did not call him his enemy. No, he called him friend. Oh yes. Even in the face of betrayal, Jesus is the friend of sinners.

Reflect

Have there been ways that you have been deceived by the love of money? Pray and ask the Lord to open your eyes and remember your death.

The Fourth Week of Lent

Tension Mounts

Monday

Three Blind Men

"What do you want me to do for you?"
(Mark 10:36, 51)

Read Mark 10:32-52

As Jesus continued on the road to Jerusalem, he took his disciples aside and "began to tell them the things that would happen to him" (Mark 10:32):

> *The Son of Man will be handed over to the chief priests and the scribes, and they will condemn him to death. Then they will hand him over to the Gentiles, and they will mock him, spit on him, flog him, and kill him, and he will rise after three days. (v 33-34)*

The rabbi they loved was saying something like *I am walking down to death row.* But the disciples were already dreaming of the benefits of being Jesus' followers, like overthrowing the Romans, new shoes, and probably lunch. They were oblivious to the weight of what Jesus was telling them. When he said he would "rise after three days," he might as well have been speaking Martian. Their hearts were already filled with the desire for power and fame, so there was no place for his story of self-sacrifice or *memento mori* to lodge.

In a shocking demonstration of pride, James and John say, "Teacher, we want you to do whatever we ask you" (v 35). What makes them think they can command Jesus? Yet merciful Jesus still invites them to voice their request. But when they demand, "Allow us to sit at your right and at your left in your glory," Jesus tries to explain to them that they don't even understand what they're asking (v 37-38).

Their loving Savior delights in giving good gifts, but they are like 13-year-old kids begging for a 3-D printer without understanding any of the costs involved. Even so, with patience Jesus explains the costs to them, and in sadly typical fashion they say *We can handle that.* Self-deceived children. Of course, when the rest of the disciples find out that James and John have jumped the gun and called dibs on the seats of honor they want, they are indignant. They are just upset because they haven't thought to ask for power and fame first.

Later, as they walked along with crowds following, a blind man named Bartimaeus was sitting by the road begging. When he heard that Jesus was heading his way, "he began to cry out, 'Jesus, Son of David, have mercy on me!'" (v 47). Of course, the people tried to hush him up. Nothing like a blind beggar to ruin a good parade. But he continued to cry out all the more, "Have mercy on me, Son of David!" (v 48).

> *Jesus stopped and said, "Call him." So they called the blind man and said to him, "Have courage! Get up; he's calling for you." He threw off his coat, jumped up, and came to Jesus. (v 49-50)*

"What do you want me to do for you?" came the question (v 51). "Rabboni," the blind man said to him, "I want to see."

> *Jesus said to him, "Go, your faith has saved you." Immediately he could see and began to follow Jesus on the road. (v 52)*

It would not be hard to draw comparisons between this desperate beggar pleading for mercy and those ambitious disciples demanding honor. And it would not be wrong for us to look at our own lives and draw that contrast either. Are we desperate for mercy or demanding glory? Good question.

But there is something even more wonderful at play here. The Lord who asked, "What do you want me to do for you?" in both instances granted the request. He granted the requests! He restored sight to Bartimaeus, and he laid down his life so that power-grubbing and spiritually blind followers like James and John (and you and me) might sit with him in his glory.

Reflect

In what ways do you resonate with James and John's request for power? In what ways do you resonate with Bartimaeus' appeal for mercy?

Tuesday

The King Weeps

"I tell you, if they were to keep silent,
the stones would cry out."
(Luke 19:40)

Read Luke 19:28-40

Jesus' arrival in Jerusalem held the promise of a bright future for some and signaled a day of doom for others. For his followers, his triumphal entry seemed to inaugurate the King's rule they longed for. So celebration ensued. The people sang:

> *Blessed is the King who comes in the name of the Lord.*
> *Peace in heaven and glory in the highest heaven!*
> *(Luke 19:38)*

These words echo both Psalm 118:26 and the angel chorus at the birth of Jesus: "Glory to God in the highest heaven and peace on earth!" (Luke 2:14). Praise from heaven and earth surrounded both Jesus' birth and death. But as much as we love those words of peace and glory, they were not yet fully realized. Yes, he did bring peace to some. And yes, his Father was glorified. But this kingdom was not yet understood nor fully inaugurated.

He was the King who came in the name of the sovereign Lord. He came to reestablish his Father's rule, to bring all creation back into alignment and flourishing. What does peace in heaven and on earth and glory to God actually look like? What kind of kingdom would accurately reflect his character? One where the religious leaders would love the people more than themselves. If only they would be willing to say "no" to their personal kingdom-building and humbly lay down their lives for the people.

It seemed like a joyous day. A donkey upon whom no one had ever ridden submitted itself to bear the burden of his weight (and to fulfill prophecy—Zechariah 9:9). Palm branches "clapped their hands" in celebration (see Isaiah 55:12). Clothing created a beautiful pathway of honor for him. Families rejoiced and cheered. The people hoped that finally, yes finally, the king they longed for had come. Jesus would make Israel great again!

Jesus understood that their hopes were skewed but did not rebuke them. He knew they longed for a king, but he also knew that their hopes weren't big enough. They wanted a political savior; he would be their perfect Messiah. Jesus also knew the pain and grief that must come before these things were accomplished. He knew that though they were dancing and rejoicing in the streets over him on this day, it would not be long before cries of "Hosanna" would be changed into shouts of "Crucify." Even so, he welcomed their praise.

Sadly, upon seeing their exuberance and hearing the cries of joy from the crowds, the leaders demanded, "Teacher, rebuke your disciples." But Jesus refused:

> *I tell you, if they were to keep silent, the stones would cry out. (Luke 19:40)*

All our praises are polluted with dreams of our own grandeur. It's easier to worship God when we expect he will give us what we want. Let's face it, the rocks would probably make a better choir. So, "as he approached and saw the city, *he wept for it*" (v 41, emphasis added). Instead of raising his arms in triumph and proclaiming, *I am a great King! Cheer for me!* he saw the people and the city for what they really were, and his heart broke. He wept. Did the cheering crowds notice his tears?

He lamented over Jerusalem (to use the words he would utter a few days later):

> *Jerusalem, Jerusalem, who kills the prophets and stones those who are sent to her. How often I wanted to gather your children together, as a hen gathers her chicks under her wings, but you were not willing! (Matthew 23:37)*

Are you willing? Will you let Jesus gather you to himself? Will you follow him by laying down your life for others? Are you willing to let his tears become your own? Are you willing to lament with him, repent from all your dreams of greatness, of being independent and strong, and let him treat you as what you really are: a weak little bird? You must not praise him because he is going to make you great or give you what you want. You cannot use him as the stairway to your own coronation. Instead, you are invited to praise him because he is the true King and, as his lowly subject, you are under his loving protection.

Reflect

Can you think of any ways that you have assumed that it was Jesus' plan to fulfill all your ambitions? How do his tears convict you? What would it look like for you to submit your plans to his today?

Wednesday

A House for All

"Zeal for your house has consumed me..."
(Psalm 69:9)

Read Matthew 21:12-17

Throughout the year, but especially on feast days, worshipers would travel to the temple in Jerusalem to offer sacrifices to the Lord. But there was a problem: the temple would not accept foreign currency, so travelers needed to exchange their money before offering it. Money-changing might have started as a helpful service, but it became an opportunity to rob the foreigner. Also, according to Mosaic law, the poor could offer birds as sacrifices. Because birds could not be easily transported, they were sold at the temple—at a little mark-up, of course.

Upon seeing this, Jesus could not stand idly by while the house of prayer was made into a den of thieves (v 13). Jesus ruined the profits of those greedy robbers by overturning the money changers' tables. He scattered them and their coins. Needless to say, his shocking actions did not ingratiate him with the religious leaders.

What would move this man of peace and gentleness to such violence? What was his problem? The priests—those who had been called to be God's representatives—were using his people's devotion to humiliate and exploit them. Jesus cared so deeply about his people that he was enraged by the state of the temple. Later, in a parable, Jesus highlighted his care for the poor, sick, and foreigner by explaining that whatever you did to "one of the least of these brothers and sisters of mine, you did for me" (25:40).

The King appeared in judgment in the temple that day, as a terrifying rain of fire and bleach scalding religious leaders and crooks alike. He referred to the prophet Isaiah, quoting a portion of Isaiah 56:

As for the foreigners who join themselves to the LORD
to minister to him, to love the name of the LORD,
and to become his servants—
all who keep the Sabbath without desecrating it
and who hold firmly to my covenant—
I will bring them to my holy mountain
and let them rejoice in my house of prayer.
Their burnt offerings and sacrifices
will be acceptable on my altar,
for my house will be called a house of prayer
for all nations. (Isaiah 56:6-7)

King Jesus defended his Father's honor and stood with the vulnerable against the greedy and powerful. Why? Because his Father loved the "foreigners" who wanted to "join themselves to the LORD," love him, and "become his servants" (v 6). God was going to bring outsiders to his "holy mountain" and "let them rejoice" in his "house of prayer." In fact, this would happen to such an extent that the temple itself, which they had filled with such thievery, would not be known as a house of prayer for pure-bloods but instead be called "a house of prayer for *all nations.*" The end for which the King was raging was that people from every nation would know they were radically welcomed into his house.

Jesus' actions that day did not transform the temple. But change would inevitably come when the temple was later destroyed, never to be rebuilt. Eventually God's invitation to the Gentiles would be heard by the entire world: *Come and pray to me! All are welcome here.* Now the global church is a fellowship of foreigners united around their love for their King, yet the temptation to build houses of worship that exclude people of different backgrounds or classes remains. Consider today what you have done lately to love and care for the "least of these," and how you can make your own church a place that welcomes all, especially the poor and vulnerable.

Reflect

What do you do to care for and protect the vulnerable? How do Jesus' actions convict or encourage you?

Thursday

More Humble than Jesus?

"I am among you as the one who serves."
(Luke 22:27)

Read John 13:1-17

Jesus and his disciples had gathered for the Passover meal. And as he knew that soon the time would come for him to return home to his Father, his heart was filled with love for his people. Now more than ever, every moment mattered. Never one to let social norms stop him from seizing a teaching moment, Jesus...

> *... got up from supper, laid aside his outer clothing, took a towel, and tied it around himself. Next, he poured water into a basin and began to wash his disciples' feet and to dry them with the towel tied around him. (v 4-5)*

It is hard for us to grasp the significance of what Jesus did that night. The task of washing a visitor's filthy feet fell to the lowliest slave in a household. After walking on dirt roads, often covered in animal refuse, visitors' feet would be caked in all sorts of stinking filth. So the humblest slave would have to kneel down to touch, smell, and wash, making the guest's filth his own.

So when *Jesus* knelt to wash, this action took the disciples' breath away. It should take ours away as well.

Never one to let confusion silence him, Peter objected: "Lord, are you going to wash my feet? … You will never wash my feet" (v 6, 8). Peter assumed that he knew what proper behavior for a King should be. Never assume you have a better understanding of anything than Jesus does. Peter loved his rabbi, but he still did not understand that Jesus' mission and kingship was one of service, not fortifying social rank and exercising power over others. Peter knew that he should kneel before his King; he could not accept that his King would kneel before him.

To Peter's objections Jesus replied, "What I'm doing you don't realize now, but afterward you will understand" (v 7). After what? What would enable Peter to understand? Yes, Jesus' death and resurrection, but also Peter's failures, bitter tears, and eventual restoration (John 21:15-19). Soon, Peter would write from a heart that had known an excruciating humiliation and, ultimately, grace:

> *All of you clothe yourselves with humility toward one another, because "God resists the proud but gives grace to the humble." Humble yourselves, therefore, under the mighty hand of God, so that he may exalt you at the proper time, casting all your cares on him, because he cares about you. (1 Peter 5:6-7)*

Peter would eventually serve his King through his own life of humble service and martyr's death. Through the process of his own humiliation, Peter would truly understand what it took for Jesus to serve him and cleanse him from all his confusion, ambition, faux humility, and pride.

Will you let Jesus serve you today? Please, no false humble objections about Jesus being too great to serve you. The King gets to decide how he interacts with his subjects, not us.

Peter did let Jesus wash his feet on that day, but he was just beginning to learn what it meant to follow his Master. Jesus said, "Truly I tell you, a servant is not greater than his master" (John 13:16). You too are called to take up the basin and the towel and serve, but only because Jesus still serves you and grants you grace. "If you know these things, you are blessed if you do them" (v 17).

Reflect

We can sometimes focus our church attendance exclusively on serving God. How might your perspective change if you saw it as a time where he serves you?

Friday

On the Night He Was Betrayed

"Truly I tell you, one of you will betray me."
(Mark 14:18)

Read Mark 14:17-25

Allow me to ask you to pause right now, before you read this day's devotion, and pray. Today, we are entering into a holy space, but it is also one that is so familiar to most of us that we will certainly be tempted to just gloss over this reading and miss the love and presence of Jesus. Ask the Spirit to awaken your heart and mind to him today.

I take communion weekly. Every week I hear Paul's words, "On the night he was betrayed..." (1 Corinthians 11:23, NIV) and I am struck. Or I should be. I should be struck by this betrayal, this best of all friends suffering at the hand of a friend. And I am also struck by how those holy words can become some common religious expression that occurs at this point in the service. "On the night... yada, yada, yada..."

But read it again: "On the night he was betrayed..."

God, have mercy. How dare we not weep at this?

On the night he was betrayed.

What is it about that word "betrayed" that signals such miserable agony? Betrayal implies broken relationship and trust. The pain of the betrayal is analogous to the depth of relationship. It is one thing for some social-media follower to diss me online. It is another thing entirely for a close family member to betray the trust I have bestowed and shame me before my enemies. Betrayal could only happen because Jesus gave himself to his disciples in friendship and relationship. He was vulnerable. He called them friends. But they were false. And yet he loved them.

Of course, Judas was the foremost betrayer, but it is not as though he was the only one that failed in friendship's obligations. The disciples all deserted Jesus. Peter denied even knowing him. They ran away and left Jesus to face his trial and torture alone. Some friends.

On the night he was betrayed.

While each of his friends tried to figure out who would betray him and boasted about the strength of their personal loyalty, Jesus was inaugurating a new sort of relationship with them and with us. This new agreement between his Father and his people would be based solely upon his love and sacrifice, not their faithfulness. From now on, all that would matter is whether you are united with Christ.

On the night he was betrayed.
He gave thanks.

On the night he was betrayed.
He took bread, blessed it, and broke it.
Take it. Eat it. This is my body, which is for you.
Remember.

On the night he was betrayed.
He held a cup for them to drink.

And they all drank from it. Betrayers and deniers alike.
This is my blood, which is poured out for many.
For you. Eat my flesh. Drink my blood.
Remember.

On the night he was betrayed.
This cup is the new covenant.
I seal it with my very blood.
I will be your God. You will be my people.

On the night he was betrayed.
He was grateful
generous
courageous
brokenhearted
and deeply faithful.

Even so…
It was night.

And so, we weep.

Reflect
When you take communion you are "proclaiming his death until he comes" (1 Corinthians 11:26). How might that proclamation change the rest of your week?

Saturday

The Power of Darkness

"This is your hour, and the power of darkness."
(Luke 22:53, NKJV)

Read Mark 14:32-42

After singing a hymn, Jesus and his disciples left the upper room and went by night to the Mount of Olives, to a garden called Gethsemane. "Sit here while I pray," he asked (v 32). Little enough to ask. *Just sit here near me.*

Then he took Peter, James, and John deeper into the garden as the gloom and the power of darkness grew. Jesus felt "deeply distressed and troubled" (v 33). These words tell us that he was alarmed and in anxiety.[9] Jesus told his best friends, "I am deeply grieved to the point of death" (v 34). Eugene Peterson paraphrased it this way:

> *He plunged into a sinkhole of dreadful agony. He told them, "I feel bad enough right now to die." (v 33-34, MSG)*

When you think about Jesus, do the words "alarmed," "in anxiety," "deeply grieved," and "feel bad enough to die" seem a bit shocking? Because Jesus is both God and man, it is easy

9 *Ekthambeisthai:* be very excited, be alarmed; *adēmonein:* be distressed, be in anxiety.

to assume that his Godhood made trials effortless for him. *Sure,* we think, *he might have had a little discomfort, but he's God. It couldn't have been that bad, right?* We could not be more wrong.

Jesus had fought the power of this darkness once before: when he was alone for 40 days in the wilderness. Think again about those temptations that began his ministry, just as these would signal its conclusion.

Would he use his power to ease the suffering of his physical body?

Would he try to force his Father's hand to save him?

Would he embrace the honors of the world and all its kingdoms, or would he instead please his Father and walk into disgrace?

Same temptations. Same result. In the wilderness, he faced down his adversary's temptations with words from the Torah that he had learned as a child. This time, in the garden, he faced down his adversary's temptations with words from the depths of his faithful soul: "Not my will, but yours, be done" (Luke 22:42). Throughout his whole life, Jesus consistently lived out these words: "Go away, Satan! For it is written: Worship the Lord your God, and serve only him" (Matthew 4:10).

Jesus did not get any special help in this battle. His friends were worse than no help at all. Three times he went to them and asked them to watch with him (26:38), but alas, they were "exhausted from their grief" (Luke 22:45), and they slept. Finally, at the end of his fight, an angel "from heaven appeared to him, strengthening him" (v 43).

This is such a perfect portrayal of who Jesus is and who we are. He is our humble warrior King, who courageously fought the power of darkness with such intensity that he sweat blood. Conversely, we are the ones who do not understand, who feel afraid and confused. Without any effort at all, the power of darkness envelops us and puts us right to sleep.

So many times, I have heard sermons about how we should say, "Not my will." And that is right… sort of. But only so if we are also reminded that the primary point of this story is that we habitually do *not* say, "Not my will." Rather, we say things like "I'll be the faithful one!" and then promptly take a nap.

Our only hope in the face of sedating darkness is that Jesus is the Light of the world. And "that light shines in the darkness, and yet the darkness did not overcome it" (John 1:5).

Yes, the power of darkness is strong. And yes, we often check out of the fight to be faithful. But take heart. He is stronger than the darkness. He vanquished it.

Reflect

How does the disciples' failure to stay awake while Christ suffered compare with your practices during this Lenten journey? How does John 1:5 comfort you when you become aware of your own flaws or lack of obedience?

The Fifth Week of Lent

The Rebellion

Monday

The Disciple Who Sold Jesus

"Friend ... why have you come?"
(Matthew 26:50)

Read Matthew 26:47-56

Judas Iscariot is infamous for one thing: betraying Jesus to death. We know that Judas loved money, stole from the common purse the disciples relied on, and spoke derisively about Mary's anointing of Jesus (John 12:4-6). On the other hand, we also know that he followed Jesus for several years, listening to his teaching and witnessing his miracles, sacrificing his comforts and ambitions to be counted among his friends. How then, do we make sense of Judas' life, his betrayal, and, ultimately, his suicide? What follows is just one way to think about him, a way that may help us understand and perhaps even give us warning.

One disciple was not sleeping that night in Gethsemane: Judas. He had been one busy bee. He had a plan. And it was finally coming together.

Ever since the disturbing scene with that woman and the perfume, Judas had begun to suspect that he might have to take matters into his own hands before Jesus blew it completely.

It was a shame. Things had been going along so swimmingly. His rabbi had been growing in popularity. The movement had been finally gaining traction. Jesus had even raised Lazarus to life after being dead for four days. No one could refuse Jesus his throne now. Then he had ridden into the city in triumph, with cheering crowds. It had all been going to plan.

But then, as if that incident with the woman and the weeping was not jarring enough, Jesus had attacked those working in the temple courts. Then he had doubled down on talk of his rejection and death, while also talking about paying taxes to the Roman occupiers. Surely now was the time to act, while the city was full of worshipers who were primed for a little rumble with the Romans. But… nothing.

The time was ripe to spark a rebellion. That might call for a little bloodshed, but nothing ever happens without some spilled blood, right? Perhaps Jesus just needed a nudge to push him over the line.

And Judas believed he was exactly the right guy for the job. So he went to the Sanhedrin and asked, *What will you give me?* (Matthew 26:15).

The answer was thirty pieces of silver. So now they were jangling in Judas' money bag, a nice little perk for all these midnight labors. Of course, perhaps he thought, he would never keep the money. No, just as soon as he forced Jesus to defend himself and claim his rightful throne, he would put the money to good use. Probably.

Then he, Judas, would forever be remembered as the one who urged the King to claim his kingdom, who moved things along by going out on a limb for his rabbi. He could see it now: *Judas: The Guy Who Knew How to Get Things Done.*

Jesus had even called him "friend" (Matthew 26:50). In his self-delusion, Judas was sure he was right. Jesus knew he could count on him. Jesus knew enough to embrace greatness when he saw it.

So Judas kissed him.

Then later, in one horrifying moment, when Judas realized that Jesus had not defended himself, had not fought back, and had been condemned to death, the light blazed, and he saw himself and the King. He saw his self-deception. He would not be remembered for his bold, clever king-making. He would be remembered for his betrayal. "It would have been better for him if he had not been born" (Mark 14:21). Darkness devoured him. And he went out and hanged himself (Matthew 27:5).

It is easy for us to think of Judas as despicable—as utterly different from us. But then his life would not teach us what it should. When we think about his story, instead of saying, "I would never!" shouldn't we ask, "When have I taken something that was not mine to take? When have I betrayed someone I had sworn loyalty to? When have I decided what is best, assumed Jesus would agree, and failed to actually listen to him?" Judas was a committed disciple who had left everything to follow his Messiah. In imagining Judas as a man not only consumed with greed but also ambition and pride, perhaps we are now more able to see that we are not that different after all.

Reflect

How have you thought about Judas in the past? How has this imagined perspective given insight into ways you might not be so different from Judas?

Tuesday

How to Arrest God

"If you're looking for me, let these men go."
(John 18:8)

Read John 18:1-11

How do you arrest God? Well, of course, you don't know it's God you're arresting, or you would never. But still.

How do you arrest God? You wait until night because you would not want to awaken the sleeping masses and start a fight. That would be trouble.

How do you arrest God? You look for a willing accomplice. Why did they need a Judas to point out who Jesus was? Jesus was already well-known to them: he had taught them daily in the temple (Mark 14:49). But it is possible for even soldiers to get confused in the dark. Better safe than sorry. You would not want to arrest just any old guy when you are hunting down God.

How do you arm yourself when you set off to arrest God? You gather "lanterns, torches, and weapons" and "swords and clubs" (John 18:3; Mark 14:43). You never know what God might do. If he were God (which, of course, he could not be, right?), it is possible that he might call on "more than twelve legions of angels" (Matthew 26:53) for defense. So, better get weaponed up. Sharpen your sword. Take a few practice swings with that club. You never know.

How many people would you need? Better take a "company of soldiers" and some "officials" (John 18:23). Bring the temple SWAT officers and a "large mob" (Matthew 26:47).

God, who knew "everything that was about to happen to him" (John 18:4), stepped out from the darkness of the garden into the light of their lanterns and asked…

"Who is it that you're seeking?"

Good question. God? Hope not. Your King? Nope. The Messiah? Doesn't look like it.

"Who is it that you're seeking?"

"Jesus of Nazareth," they answered…

"I am he."

When Jesus told them, "I am he," they stepped back and fell to the ground. (v 4-5, 6)

Wait a minute. Who *is* this?

His courage made their knees buckle. They fell back like weak children—a proper posture when speaking to God. Still, because God was committed to following through on his plan, he made it easy for them, sprawled in disarray all over the ground as they were, and asked again:

"Who is it that you're seeking?"

Jesus, God's only begotten Son? No. Just some radical from Nazareth. A loser rabbi from a loser village.

"I told you I am he," Jesus replied. "So if you're looking for me, let these men go." (v 7-8)

Here, in Gethsemane, his favorite sanctuary, on the night

when his disciples slept and his friend betrayed, Jesus offered himself. "Let these men go." The question of whether he would do this or not had already been settled: "Not my will, but yours, be done" (Luke 22:42).

Anyone would have expected a king to take this opportunity to accuse Judas or try to escape or tell his disciples to fight. But that's not how God acted. God said, "Let these men go."

Do what? "Let these men go." God allowed the soldiers to seize him as if he were a common criminal. The holy untouchable God allowed himself to be dragged away to trial so the guilty would go free.

How do you arrest God? You don't. Not unless he lets you. Why would he? Because he loves. He allowed himself to be temporarily imprisoned that you might be free from every deserved charge of unlawfulness, folly, cowardice, laziness, disinterestedness, or pride that might be brought against you. God allowed them to arrest him. He became the criminal so that we can escape as the innocents.

Oh, and on his way out, God healed a slave's ear. Of course he did. He would not make a slave shed blood for Peter's rash folly. His blood was all that would be necessary in these hours. "Put your sword away" (John 18:11), Jesus told Peter. Jesus would not be the kind of king whose kingdom would be built on violence against the weak and on the suffering of a slave. No, shedding blood and suffering was what now lay before God. So when they asked him who he was, he responded, "I am he."

Reflect

Jesus' question to the mob is one for us to consider, too. Who are you seeking? How do you respond when Jesus doesn't meet your expectations of him?

Wednesday

Why Did You Strike Me?

"'If I have spoken wrongly,' Jesus answered him, 'give evidence about the wrong; but if rightly, why do you hit me?'"
(John 18:23)

Read Matthew 26:57-64

"The chief priests and the whole Sanhedrin were looking for false testimony against Jesus so that they could put him to death" (Matthew 26:59). The goal of their nighttime gathering had been predetermined: Jesus' execution. But they had to pretend to have a fair trial. So they hired men to give false evidence. We might assume that priests who served the God who commanded, "Do not give false testimony against your neighbor" (Exodus 20:16) would have noticed that they themselves were now the guilty ones.

Indeed, they were guilty of the serial violation of many of God's commandments. They could not see how they had fashioned idols out of their places of honor, how they had falsely claimed God's name for themselves, nor how they never rested in the kindness God had bestowed upon them in the Sabbath and instead used the command to rest as a whip to make others work. Hence, it was nothing for them to steal this man's good name. Murder in the name of false righteousness? How blind do you have to be to arrange to kill the Son of God? How ambitious do you have to be to strike him, perhaps assuming you are doing God (and your boss) a favor?

After his arrest, Jesus stood trial before the high priest and his council. They heard the false testimonies. Finally, fearing that the proceeding was getting away from him, the high priest took the matter into his own hands, asking Jesus about his teaching. Jesus replied that there were many others who had heard him. He should ask them. Unlike these liars, they would tell him the truth.

> *When he had said these things, one of the officials standing by slapped Jesus, saying, "Is this the way you answer the high priest?"" (John 18:22)*

Concerned about proper respect for his boss, an official slapped Jesus and rebuked him. It is nice when you get an opportunity to prove your allegiance to the higher-ups, right? You never know when that promotion you have been wanting might come along. Thankfully, now he would forever be remembered as a zealous bureaucrat who was willing to act.

"Is this the way you answer the high priest?" he asked. And he slapped Jesus.

He slapped Jesus. Let that sink in. Never underestimate the corrupting power of misplaced loyalty and ambition. To him Jesus responded:

> *"If I have spoken wrongly … give evidence about the wrong; but if rightly, why do you strike me?" (John 18:23)*

Why indeed.

About 700 years before this unnamed bureaucrat kissed up to his boss, Isaiah the prophet foretold his action. Jesus…

... was cut off from the land of the living; ***he was struck because of my people's rebellion.***

(Isaiah 53:8, emphasis added)

And so it had begun: this was just the first of many blows that would soon become a torrent raining down upon Jesus' head. This first blow was struck by an insignificant cog in his own people's religious machinery.

He was struck because of my people's rebellion.

Did the religious leaders know they were fulfilling Scripture? Of course not. They thought they were protecting God's kingdom from polluting heresy, missing the fact that they were the ones who were in rebellion against God. And yet, this unnamed bureaucrat fulfilled Scripture.

He was struck because of my people's rebellion.

The entire council had rebelled against loyal love. And yet, they fulfilled Isaiah's prophecy:

He was struck because of my people's rebellion.

Finally, the high priest asked Jesus, "Are you the Messiah, the Son of the Blessed One?"

"I am," said Jesus (Mark 14:61-62).

And so it was settled.

"He deserves death!" (Matthew 26:66)

Then they spit in his face.

Strange water to anoint a King, isn't it?

Reflect

Consider what Jesus went through for you, even before he was nailed to the cross for you. How does it make you feel? In what way will you respond?

Thursday

A Lesson About Listening

"I have prayed for you that your faith may not fail."
(Luke 22:31)

Read Luke 22:31-46, 54-62

On the night when Judas kept his promise to betray his friend, Simon Peter was fast asleep. And no wonder. The last few days had been an exhausting emotional roller coaster. Peter went from experiencing the cheering crowds as they sang their hosannas and waved palm branches to seeing Jesus overturn tables in the temple courts. When Jesus stooped to wash his feet, Peter refused; then, when Jesus insisted, he asked for his hands and head to be cleaned as well. This was not the series of events Peter had expected when they arrived in Jerusalem for the Passover.

But as surprising as all of this probably was, it was nothing in comparison to the predictions Jesus had made about his friends. "All of you will fall away, because it is written: 'I will strike the shepherd, and the sheep will be scattered'" (Mark 14:27). Wait. What? The disciples would be scattered? They would have probably thought it was impossible. Peter certainly did (Mark 14:29).

No one will argue with the fact that Peter was impetuous and headstrong. He was a man with an opinion about everything, and he was not shy about sharing it. He was always speaking and acting before listening or thinking. Once, on the Mount of Transfiguration, when Moses and Elijah appeared with Jesus, the three disciples present—Peter among them—were terrified into silence. But then, Mark writes, "he did not know what to say, since they were terrified" (Mark 9:6). Instead of letting his fear silence him, Peter decided he knew what to do. So incessant was his talking that it was stopped only when God the Father himself spoke to him from heaven: "This is my beloved Son; listen to him!" (Mark 9:7).

Simon Peter would have been wise to recall those words when the beloved Son told his friends that they would all desert him. Did he listen to him? No. He refused to and declared his faithfulness. So Jesus persisted: "Simon, Simon, look out. Satan has asked to sift you like wheat. But I have prayed for you that your faith may not fail" (Luke 22:31).

Did Peter hear that the only thing that stopped his utter destruction were the prayers of his friend? Did he listen? No. All Peter could hear was his own voice. "'Lord,' he told [Jesus], 'I'm ready to go with you both to prison and to death.'" Was he? Hardly. This courage would fail within hours. And so, because he loved his friend, Jesus once more persisted and told him exactly how the night would go: "I tell you, Peter … the rooster will not crow today until you deny three times that you know me" (Luke 22:34).

What was Peter's response? Did he listen? Did he repent or plead for help? No. He thought Jesus was wrong. And because Peter was a man completely convinced of his strength, prayer to resist temptation was nowhere on his list. Like all self-assured people, he thought he did not need to pray. Later, Peter and his friends would sleep rather than pray because, though they were "exhausted from their grief" (Luke 22:45), they were also convinced they had the strength to persevere.

Then came Judas' kiss and Jesus' arrest and "all the disciples deserted him and ran away" (Matthew 26:56)—except Peter, who followed along at a distance and then warmed himself by a fire in the high priest's courtyard. Perhaps Peter thought that he would be the one disciple to prove faithful. Perhaps he saw this as the moment to show how wrong Jesus had been. But then…

> *A servant girl approached him and said, "You were with Jesus the Galilean too." But he denied it in front of everyone: "I don't know what you're talking about."*
>
> *When he had gone out to the gateway, another woman saw him and told those who were there, "This man was with Jesus the Nazarene!"*
>
> *And again he denied it with an oath: "I don't know the man!"*
>
> *After a little while those standing there approached and said to Peter, "You really are one of them, since even your accent gives you away."*
>
> *Then he started to curse and to swear with an oath, "I don't know the man!" (Matthew 26:69-74)*

And then finally Peter listened as the rooster spoke. He saw himself, perhaps for the first time. And Jesus walked through the courtyard and "turned and looked at Peter" (Luke 22:61).

Jesus made certain that Peter knew that he saw him, too.

Peter went out and wept bitterly.

Good thing one of them had remained loyal. Good thing one of them had prayed.

Reflect

It is easy to see the ways that Peter failed. Are you convinced enough of Jesus' love for you that you are willing to see and confess your own failures?

Friday

Who Are You?

"Look, the Lamb of God, who
takes away the sin of the world!"
(John 1:29)

Read John 18:28-38

The time had come to bind the sacrifice before it was offered. Hands that had just washed feet, broken bread, and healed were bound. Jesus was led from the headquarters of religious power to Pilate, the empire's representative.

The religious leaders needed to converse with Pilate, but they had a problem: they could not enter the "headquarters themselves; otherwise they would be defiled and unable to eat the Passover" (John 18:28). When you are arranging the assassination of the Lamb of God on the eve of Passover, you must avoid disqualifying defilement. So Pilate came out to them.

He asked Jesus a series of questions. To his question, "So You are the King of the Jews?" Jesus answered, "It is as you say" (Matthew 27:11, NASB). When he asked, "Don't you hear how much they are testifying against you?" (v 13), Jesus gave no reply.

But to Pilate's question, "What have you done?" Jesus answered, "My kingdom is not of this world … If my kingdom were of this world, my servants would fight … But as it is, my kingdom is not from here" (John 18:36). Jesus had brought their charges upon himself by disdaining their kingdom. And they would not tolerate anyone questioning the power of Rome.

Generally, the Lamb of God "did not open his mouth" (Isaiah 53:7), but to Pilate's query, "You are a king then?" Jesus responded:

> *I was born for this, and I have come into the world for this: to testify to the truth. Everyone who is of the truth listens to my voice. (John 18:37)*

Pilate concluded the conversation with one question:

> *What is truth? (John 18:38)*

Good question. Jesus, the King of truth, is standing bound, right before his eyes. Does he really want to know what truth is, or is he just rehearsing some old philosophical question he presumes has no answer? Because Jesus did not respond to him, we might assume the latter.

According to the Gospel of Luke, Jesus was then sent to King Herod. Herod was a coarse despot who loved a good party. He had really enjoyed his stepdaughter's dance. Sure, her request for John the Baptist's bloody head on a plate brought things down for a moment (see Mark 6:17-28). But still. The wine flowed and the merrymaking continued. After all, in a boring place like Jerusalem, there were not a lot of options for entertainment. So, Herod was…

> *… very glad to see Jesus; for a long time he had wanted to see him because he had heard about him and was hoping to see some miracle performed by him. (Luke 23:8)*

This vicious tyrant's response to Jesus could be summarized in this way: *Amuse me, monkey!* The reason Herod was happy to see Jesus was not because he was looking for truth or salvation. No. He just needed something to distract and divert him. And one can only drink so much wine.

When Jesus refused, Herod, "with his soldiers, treated him with contempt, mocked him, dressed him in bright clothing, and sent him back to Pilate" (Luke 23:11). King Jesus, the circus clown.

Both Pilate and Herod, powerful men, were facing one question: *Who is this?* Is he a blasphemer to be rejected, a philosopher to be drawn into pointless philosophical discussions, or a clown for today's entertainment? Or is he the Lamb of God, sent to take away the sins of the world (John 1:29)? The three typical representatives of religion, government, and base entertainment each got the answer wrong. Do we?

You probably know how you *should* answer that question. But is that how you live? Do you see Jesus primarily as the one who came to bear away all your failures and faults, the King under whose rule you arrange your life? Or is he merely an interesting topic of discussion, someone to amuse you, or a fun diversion? Is he a novel philosopher, a circus clown, or God's sacrificial Lamb?

Even as our reigning King, Jesus continues to bear away all our punishment for every time we have answered questions about his identity wrongly. Thank God.

Reflect

How does, or how should, Jesus' title of "Lamb of God" impact your daily life?

Saturday

To Choose Not to Choose Is a Choice

""I am innocent of this man's blood"
(Matthew 27:24)

Read Matthew 27:15-26

Pilate had already concluded that Jesus was innocent (John 18:38). Jesus' quiet demeanor and answers had troubled him deeply. When his wife warned him, "Have nothing to do with that righteous man" (Matthew 27:19), he grew even more concerned over the dilemma before him.

Pilate was under pressure from Rome, the zealots, and the Pharisees, but he did try to be fair. He would not want to condemn an obviously innocent man, but he also would not want Rome to think he was failing to protect the empire. Eventually, he came up with a clever idea: he would let the people choose a prisoner to be released. He probably didn't think there was any chance the people would choose Barabbas, that notorious murderer.

Perhaps Pilate's thoughts went like this: *That should work. Will it be Jesus' or Barabbas' lucky day? The people (and the gods) will decide.* In any case, it was out of his hands. Whew! This plan was political expediency at its best; whatever way it went, he would be innocent. If the crowds wanted Jesus released, and the Pharisees were vexed, so much the better. But, if, on the other hand, the crowd demanded Jesus' death, then when his conscience (or his wife) nagged him, Pilate could honestly say, *It wasn't the choice I would have made, but what could I do?* So, he let the people vote; he was nothing more than an innocent bystander.

In their envy, the religious leaders stirred up the crowds to demand that Pilate release Barabbas (Matthew 27:20). "What should I do then with Jesus, who is called Christ?" asked the governor. And the crowd chanted, "Crucify him!"

Pilate asked again, "Why, what has he done … ?" We know that answer. We have considered it for days: he has welcomed, he has healed, he has delivered, he has protected, he has forgiven, he has raised the dead. What had he done? He had dared to speak the truth. What had Barabbas done? Led a murderous rebellion. Was there any justice in this world?

Pilate probably hated to think about himself as unjust. Whatever humanity was left within him still longed to believe in his own goodness and show he was not blameworthy in this circumstance. So, in a visual demonstration of his innocence in the matter, he washed his hands in front of the crowd. See? He was clean. This was not his fault. He was guiltless.

It had only been a few hours since Jesus himself had had his hands in a basin of water. He had washed his disciples' feet. The humble servant-King knelt before his followers to wash their feet and demonstrate that a life of following him was a life of service. Jesus was already clean, and he was about to offer himself as a sacrifice to cleanse all who would follow him. But now Pilate had his hands in a basin and was vainly trying to cleanse himself and make himself innocent. It wouldn't work.

There is only one fluid that is powerful enough to wash away guilt, and it isn't water. It is blood. And not just any blood—only the sacrifice of innocent blood can atone for sin. So, go ahead, Pilate. Wash your hands. It won't help. There's not enough water in the world to free you from the guilt of this choice. Yes, you are guilty, because refusing to choose is to choose. So, scrub away. Water will not help you grow a backbone, nor will it silence your conscience.

"I am innocent of this man's blood" he falsely proclaimed.

All the people answered, "His blood be on us and on our children!" (Matthew 27:25)

Yes and amen to that. Let his blood be on us and on our children. There is enough innocent blood in Jesus to cleanse us all. And we need it. We need it for every time that we proudly choose to do wrong, and for every time that we allow wrong when it is in our power to stop it. We need it for every time that we have oh-so-cleverly avoided hard choices and lied to ourselves that the injustice and sin were not our fault. We need it for every time we have vainly proclaimed our innocence. Amen, wash us, Lord. Let your blood be on us.

Reflect

Can you think of any time when you chose not to choose, or made someone else choose for you? What made you do it?

Holy Week

A Scandalous Coronation

Monday

Behold the Man

"Now since the children have flesh and blood in common, Jesus also shared in these..."
(Hebrews 2:14)

Read John 19:1-5

Some thirty years before the events we've been considering, a tiny embryo had miraculously grown within the uterus of a young virgin. Within her frail body, a person with a beating heart, skin, bones, and a face was formed.

Soon, her baby entered our world and breathed our air. He learned to suckle and cry when he was in need. He was taught language, and as he grew, he learned the Torah from his earthly father and his local rabbi. Yes, he was a sweet child, but he did not appear to be anything special. He grew up in a poor household and learned a trade from his dad. At some point after his 12th birthday, his father Joseph died, so he assumed leadership in the home. He knew what it was to work six days a week to provide food for his mother and his siblings in their little village.

He looked completely ordinary in the three decades prior to his baptism by his cousin John. When he walked down the street, he would go unnoticed.

At around thirty years old, he began a public ministry. He was both loved and hated. Women bowed before him in worship, and men gave up everything to follow him. He infuriated the rulers of his people, and finally his life ended in the way it had started: naked, bloody, and in poverty and shame. Not even the deep love his mother felt for her son as she nursed him on the night of his birth would be strong enough to protect him from the life of suffering before him.

Who was this man? Pontius Pilate unwittingly invites us to look. Jesus had already endured several beatings and had been crowned with thorns and dressed in kingly robes when Pilate pronounced, *Ecce homo*—"Here is the man!" (John 19:5).

I have a reproduction of a painting of this scene in my house. In 1871 Antonio Ciseri painted *Ecce Homo*. It depicts Pilate pointing Jesus out and various people either looking at him or turning away.

Perhaps, by having Jesus stand before the crowds, bloodied, wearing thorns on his head, in faux regalia, Pilate was trying to prove that Jesus really wasn't a threat. He wasn't any big deal. *Look at his body. See? He bleeds. He's a nothing. He's let us beat him. He couldn't stop us from mocking him by dressing him in a kingly robe. "Behold the man." He's just a man. Just a normal Joe. "Ecce homo." He's just like you. He's nothing. No one.*

Certainly, if you had been in the crowd that day and had seen that half-naked body, bruised and bloodied as it was, you too would have thought he was just a man. Yes, perhaps a good teacher, but still… If you had been one of his followers, you would have heard the teaching and have been astonished by his wisdom, but wise teachers have come and gone throughout human history. *Just a man.* Yes, there were those mystifying miracles. He fed thousands; he healed the sick; he cast out demons, controlled the weather, and walked on water. He even raised the dead. But generally speaking, aside from those flashes of glory, he was just like them.

Behold the man.

He got tired. He was finite and needed to sleep, even if it was in the middle of a storm at the back of a boat. He felt hunger and thirst. After being pressed upon by crowds, in exhaustion he needed privacy and time to rest with his Father. He had a normal human body. He experienced pain the way you do. When he was slapped or beaten, he felt it.

Behold the man.

I keep my reproduction of *Ecce Homo* to remind me. Sometimes I look. Mostly I don't notice. Sometimes I wonder if it needs dusting.

Pilate's words still invite us to look today. The Spirit invites us to see. Will you take a moment to behold? Or will you look away in boredom or unbelief or disgust?

Will you behold this man?

Will you see the Christ?

Reflect

Do you ever wonder whether you are loved? How can you behold Jesus when that happens?

Tuesday

An Ordinary Day

*"And they began to salute him,
'Hail, king of the Jews!'"
(Mark 15:18)*

Read Matthew 27:27-31; Mark 15:16-20

Pilate had tried to release Jesus, and now he washed his hands. He was done. So, he gave Jesus over to his own soldiers and they…

> *… stripped him and dressed him in a scarlet robe. They twisted together a crown of thorns, put it on his head, and placed a staff in his right hand. And they knelt down before him and mocked him: "Hail, king of the Jews!" Then they spat on him, took the staff, and kept hitting him on the head. After they had mocked him, they stripped him of the robe, put his own clothes on him, and led him away to crucify him. (Matthew 27:28-31)*

When I read about these soldiers' actions, I wonder what kind of person would be comfortable inflicting that sort of pain. I wonder why they would think it was amusing to strip Jesus naked and why they enjoyed kneeling before him, clothing him in a scarlet robe. I wonder who the clever person was who twisted together a crown of thorns and thrust it down on his head, and whether he injured himself at all in his handiwork. I wonder why the soldiers would mock Jesus, and spit on him, and hit his head repeatedly with a staff. I wonder who was nominated to do the flogging that day, and if this was their typical assignment, and how one would become proficient at tearing the skin off of a person's back. I wonder why they were entertained by his weakness and his body as it bled before them. What kind of human would do such a thing?

We tend to see people as either superheroes or super-villains, so it would be easy to view these soldiers as being extra evil, completely devoid of any humanity at all. And perhaps they were—and if that's the truth, I can't see any way that I would ever be like them. But what if… what if they were just ordinary people like me? What if they were everyday soldiers, following orders and getting caught up in a mob mentality? What if they had lived so long away from loving family that they had forgotten their humanity? What if they had gladly joined the Legions early in their lives and had seen so much bloodshed that they no longer asked questions about mercy or justice or goodness? What if their hearts had been beaten so often that they no longer experienced pain in their hearts at all?

How many times have you heard the testimony of soldiers who thought what they were doing was right and ultimately for the good of their beloved country? Whether a soldier in a modern war machine or a legionary preserving the peace of Roman rule, they probably thought of themselves as good people, doing the hard but necessary things to protect the nation and the people they loved. Following orders was right and good—a way to live with honor.

And if these soldiers ever questioned their orders, they probably also felt they had no other option. Cruelty was simply part of the job; and when cruelty becomes commonplace, it stops seeming like cruelty. This was just another Friday in Palestine.

Perhaps I can bring this a little closer to home. Have you ever found yourself participating in an activity with a group of other people, finding yourself caught up in the fervor of the crowd? Ever done something you suspected was wrong, but felt you had no other option? Ever felt queasy about how someone was being treated next to or near to you, but didn't feel you could do anything other than let it happen—after all, who were you to challenge the status quo or the higher-ups? Imagine, then, that you are a soldier and all your brothers are running out to the courtyard to obey the order to flog a pretender to Caesar's throne. What would you do? Would you stand against the cruelty or join in? I wonder about those soldiers, and I start to see that, maybe, they're not so different from me.

> *After they had mocked him, they stripped him of the robe, put his own clothes on him, and led him away to crucify him. (v 31)*

Reflect

Have you ever participated in something you suspected was wrong but went along with the group anyway? What was your motivation?

Wednesday

Down Among Golgotha's Scoffers

"'He saved others,' they said,
'but he can't save himself!'"
(Mark 15:31, NIV)

Read Psalm 22

Down from Pilate's headquarters, down from the blood-soaked ground where Rome's patriots amused themselves with whips and thorns, down Jesus stumbled under the crossbeam's weight. But now, as he stumbled, perhaps the soldiers wondered if they had gotten a little carried away with the flogging. Oh well… they knew how to fix that problem. There was no shortage of bystanders who could be conscripted to serve Rome's demands. The soldiers searched the crowd for a likely candidate, and they "seized Simon from Cyrene … and put the cross on him and made him carry it behind Jesus" (Luke 23:26, NIV).

We are not told why this North African man was in the crowd that day. Perhaps he was a convert to Judaism and had just made it to the city in time to celebrate the feast of Passover. Or maybe he was just in the wrong place at the wrong time, and because he looked strong enough to carry a 32-pound beam, it was thrust upon his back. He had no choice but to obey. And so down from the city and up the little hill by the garbage dump, he carried Jesus' cross.

Did Simon know whose cross he carried? Did he stay to watch while Jesus was hammered up? We don't know. He may have left as soon as he was able. What we do know is that there were plenty of witnesses to Jesus' execution.

The friend of sinners was surrounded that day by enemies. He would have befriended them; he had desired to have gathered them under his wings (Matthew 23:37), but they had proven they were not willing. And so, those who should have joined the women who were weeping and loving and pleading for Jesus' release (and who we will consider further tomorrow) were filled with hatred and glee as they watched Jesus suffer.

> *Those who passed by were yelling insults at him, shaking their heads, and saying, "Ha! The one who would destroy the temple and rebuild it in three days, save yourself by coming down from the cross!" In the same way, the chief priests with the scribes were mocking him among themselves and saying, "He saved others, but he cannot save himself! Let the Messiah, the King of Israel, come down now from the cross, so that we may see and believe."*
>
> *(Mark 15:29-32a)*

It's hard to imagine that level of cruelty. Or is it? Using someone's own words to mock their downfall is not that unthinkable, is it? *You think you can destroy a temple and rebuild it in three days? Great! Come down from that cross and save yourself!*

Jesus heard their words of mocking and glee. They did not understand that in killing him they were actually in the process of fulfilling his prophecy: "Destroy this temple, and

I will raise it up in three days" (John 2:19). They did not understand that they were destroying Israel's true temple, or that his refusal to grasp power and save himself was for their salvation. These priests were murdering their Priest; these teachers of the law were crucifying the only law-keeper among them. They knew he had saved others. They knew he had performed miracles. But they did not care. "Save yourself!" they taunted. All Jesus had to do was prove that Jesus was who he said he was, and then they'd believe. But would they, really?

The question of who was going to be saved that day had already been asked and answered in Gethsemane when our Friend said yes to our salvation and no to his own. Now he would be lifted up, just as he had said (John 3:14). Was this filthy cross in a garbage dump a fitting throne for the friend of sinners? Of course it was. Because this is where his sinful friends belonged, and he would join them there. "Save yourself," they taunted. He would not. He was busy making salvation possible for the world.

Reflect

Surrounding Christ's cross were a mix of people: weeping believing women, Simon the Cyrene, the religious elite who mocked, the Roman soldiers who counted time till they could return to their barracks. Which group(s) does your life most resemble?

Thursday

On the Via Dolorosa

"A large crowd of people followed him, including women who were mourning and lamenting him."
(Luke 23:27)

Read Luke 21:20-24

What must it have been like to be one of those women?

It had only been five days. Five days since our mouths were filled with song! "Hosanna! Blessed is the King, who comes in the name of the Lord!" We had watched as he chased the thieves from the temple courts. This was his Father's house. He held it in honor. They had polluted it. So, he set it right. We loved our Warrior King!

He had eaten the Passover and washed the feet of his men. He had given them bread and wine and said, "Eat my body. Drink my blood." That was bizarre, but then sometimes he was just like that. And he had said he would be betrayed. Then he had returned to pray near the olive trees.

We prayed when we heard that he had been arrested by the high priest's guards. He was our King. How could they arrest him? And then we heard that he had been taken to the governor's mansion.

Maybe Pilate would release him? Then we heard that Pilate had sent him to Herod. Maybe now?

But then we heard it: "Crucify! Crucify!" And we knew. Pilate washed his hands, the Pharisees gloated, the soldiers beat him and beat him. And beat him. And then they led him out to walk the road of sorrows, a road and a life he knew so well, up to his execution.

What had they done to him? Was that even him? Oh, dear God, it was. Was this the face of the friend who had looked upon us with love? Oh, dear God, it was. And so we lined up, along the road. The disciples hid, but we would not leave him. And we wept. We held each other, and we wept.

Who was there, weeping as they followed their friend, their King, now a man condemned to be crucified? Who were these women?

Perhaps Joanna, whose husband was part of Herod's political machine but who had chosen to follow this penniless preacher.

Perhaps Martha and her sister Mary—Mary, who had in some way foreseen this and anointed him for burial. He had brought life back to their beloved brother, Lazarus. How could it be that his would be taken now?

Perhaps Veronica, a woman he called "Daughter," who was all too familiar with the sight of blood and who could now see it coming from his lacerated back and bleeding head.

Perhaps Jairus' wife and daughter were there too. Perhaps the widow of Nain. Both had seen Jesus raise others from death. Now he walked toward his own. How could it be?

Then surely there was Mary of Magdala. She thought she had known darkness before. But this… were those demons laughing again? Would evil win?

And there with her son, as she was at the beginning, was his mother, of course. Every question about her allegiance to

Jesus as God's King had been answered in Mary's heart long ago. It was always "Your will be done." But this? This? How could this be God's will?

The women all stood there weeping, sobbing for the one man who had loved them in purity and power. Confusion and terror filled their hearts.

And he looked at them, and spoke. But he did not say, *Thank you. It'll be okay. You'll see. Soon, I'll rise from the dead. Everything will work out.*

No—he said:

> *Daughters of Jerusalem, do not weep for me, but weep for yourselves and your children. Look, the days are coming when they will say, "Blessed are the women without children, the wombs that never bore, and the breasts that never nursed!" Then they will begin to say to the mountains, "Fall on us!" and to the hills, "Cover us!" (Luke 23:27-31)*

Memento mori, dear sisters. Remember you are dust and to dust you shall return, my brothers. Yes, of course, all will eventually be well. But for now, for this moment, beat your breast and weep. This is how the world treated its Maker. This is how people treat their King. There is a place for tears. For if they did this when their King was with them, what will they do when he is gone?

Reflect

Why is memento mori a wise and helpful response to shattered dreams?

Good Friday

Veiled in Flesh the Godhead See

"They will look at the one they pierced."
(John 19:37)

Read Luke 21:20-24

John quoted Zechariah the prophet: "They will look at the one they pierced" (John 19:37). So here we are: at Jesus' crucifixion, at his death. And we are faced with one question:

Will you look at the one they pierced?

I don't mean, will you look at some jewel-encrusted cross or piece of art? Nor do I mean, will you take a cross and slap it on your car's back window as a statement of your conservative values, or wear it on your T-shirt so people will know how you identify?

No. I mean, will you look, really look, at the one they pierced? Will you see his body pulverized by blow after blow from the Roman soldiers? Will you see his heart crushed by the ambition, hypocrisy, and pitiless pride that drove the religious leaders? Will you see his soul shattered as his closest followers misunderstood and chased after power and fame and safety and then deserted him and fled into the night? Will you watch as Judas kisses him, and hear Peter's denials?

Will you dare to continue to look on when even his Father looks away? As he hung there—naked, pinioned between heaven and earth, in excruciating pain—he looked up for his Father's reassuring smile and saw… nothing. And so, in despair he cried:

> *My God, my God, why have you abandoned me?*
> *(Matthew 27:46)*

After all these years of his Father's reassuring assurance, of "[You are] my beloved Son, with whom I am well-pleased" (Matthew 3:17), there was nothing. No words of familial encouragement or love. No hope. "Why?" Why indeed. Because "it was the LORD's good plan to crush him and cause him grief" (Isaiah 53:10, NLT). But again, why?

> *He was pierced for our rebellion, crushed for our sins.*
> *He was beaten so we could be whole.*
> *He was whipped so we could be healed.*
> *All of us, like sheep, have strayed away.*
> *We have left God's paths to follow our own.*
> *Yet the LORD laid on him the sins of us all. (v 5-6, NLT)*

So now, will you look? He was abandoned as a sinner so we sinners would never be. Will you see what the sin you ignore or coddle or hide or love has done? Is this enough to make you turn? Are you brave enough to stand transparently before the Father, who loves you this much, yes, so, so much, and say, "Yes, I will look"?

Or will you be like the millions Isaiah foretold, who turn their backs on him and look the other way (v 3)?

Veiled in torn and bleeding flesh, the Godhead see! Hail the incarnate dying Deity!

Will you listen as this man recognizes his need for moisture to relieve his parched throat? "I thirst." Can you hear the Son as he provides for the woman whose body carried his? "Behold your mother." Can you hear the Savior as he pleads for mercy for us all? "Forgive them, because they do not know what they are doing."

Will you listen as a condemned criminal asks the man dying by his side, "Jesus, remember me when you come into your kingdom" (Luke 23:42)—and hears this promise: "Today you will be with me in paradise" (v 43). Will you marvel that, in that promise, Jesus assured the man that he would be remembered and that he mattered—that God had always had a plan to bring that man to himself, and so it was that he finally had met the Lord who was friend of sinners to the very last.

Will you finally rest in the declaration that we are now forever his? "It is finished." Jesus knew the name of this unnamed criminal because Jesus was not only his King but his Shepherd, the one upon whose hands that man's name had been inscribed (Isaiah 49:14-16). God would never forget that criminal. And he will never forget you.

The Roman soldier looked. And he declared, "This man really was righteous!" (Luke 23:47). Yes. He was. And now, so are we.

So, again, I ask you: will you look—I mean really *look*—at the one we pierced and see him for who he is: your pierced King, who did it all for love of you?

When he breathed his last and all the strength of his flesh poured out as a river of blood and water on the earth, creation looked, and it recoiled. How could it not? The earth shuddered. The sun turned away.

Don't be afraid to look. See yourself, and see your King.

Reflect

Before you put the book down and rush on with your day, stop to spend time looking at your King, and worshiping him.

Saturday

The King Is Dead

"'He will reign over the house of Jacob forever, and his kingdom will have no end.' Mary asked the angel, 'How can this be...?'"
(Luke 1:33-34)

Read Mark 15:42-47

The Sabbath was upon them, so both Jesus' friends and his enemies were in a bind. Once the sun went down, everything had to stop. Joseph of Arimathea and Nicodemus (the Pharisee to whom Jesus had said, "You must be born again") had watched Jesus' crucifixion and death from afar. His lifeless body had to be taken down and placed in a tomb. So they went quickly to Pilate and asked for permission to dispose of it. Pilate was shocked that Jesus was already dead, and gave Jesus' body to them.

Fortunately, Joseph owned an unused tomb in a garden near Golgotha. These men, who had been so silent and inert during his trial, finally acted. They took his body and covered it with linen strips interspersed with 75 pounds of decay-slowing, odor-masking spices (John 19:39). That would have to do for the time being. Rush! The sun was setting.

Though Joseph and Nicodemus had been cowards during Jesus' life, they cared for him extravagantly in his death. Though they had loved the approval of man more than the approval of God (John 12:43), now they defied the religious leaders to make sure Jesus' body received the burial he deserved before the Sabbath came. In choosing this way, they stood against the injustice enacted by their peers, bravely identified instead with the crucified King, and surely sacrificed their positions of prestige. What had been cowardice and man-pleasing became courage and love for the Savior.

The religious leaders hoped that Jesus' death would mark the end of their trouble. But then they heard that Joseph and Nicodemus had taken his body to a tomb. Perhaps they had hoped it would have been lumped together with the other two criminals and dumped in some undesignated plot of land. But now fear began to grow within them again. Joseph and Nicodemus would probably tell Jesus' followers where his body was. They remembered that he had said he would rise again (Matthew 27:63). Who knows what that rabble who followed him would do now?

So the Pharisees, too, hurriedly visited Pilate, telling him that they needed soldiers to guard the tomb and a stone placed to stop the disciples from stealing his body (v 64). Once again, Pilate acquiesced to their requests. The religious leaders probably spent the Sabbath in fear, counting the seconds until they could assure themselves that this dangerous pretender had finally been silenced.

The women whom Jesus had called and welcomed spent the Sabbath within their homes, preparing linen and spices to swaddle his body (Luke 23:56). They hadn't had time to do what love and honor demanded of them. So Mary Magdalene and her friends made their preparations, and likely wept as they did. They waited until Sabbath was over to walk to the tomb. They would care for his body. How many tears could they shed? Was there a time when their bodies would fail to produce more? They folded cloth and cried.

Simon Peter surely spent the Sabbath in darkness, covered in despair and shame. Was he Cephas, the rock? Hardly. He was no rock. He had sworn he would never deny Jesus right before he swore he did not know him. And then Jesus had looked at him (Luke 22:61). He had known. Peter spent the Sabbath in self-awareness and shame.

Mother Mary had once seen Jesus take his first breaths. Now she had just seen him take his last. He was beyond her ability to comfort now. In her heart, surely she pondered the angel's words to her from so long ago:

> *You will conceive and give birth to a son, and you will name him Jesus. He will be great and will be called the Son of the Most High, and the Lord God will give him the throne of his father David. He will reign over the house of Jacob forever, and his kingdom will have no end.*
>
> *(Luke 1:31-33)*

Mary spent the Sabbath mourning that her son lay cold in a tomb, and perhaps remembering the promise that that son would reign "forever" over "a kingdom [with] no end" (v 33). And perhaps she asked again what she had once asked that angel all those years before: how could these things be?

And her Son, the King, spent this day in death.

Reflect

Have you ever wondered, "How could these things be?" when you considered Jesus' promises and your circumstances? How do the realities of the first Easter weekend help you wrestle with that question with faith?

Easter Sunday

What Do You Hear?

"Peace be with you."
(John 20:19)

Read John 20:1-22

We cannot hear the Father command, *My beloved Son. Arise! Welcome to the kingdom I bestow upon you.*

We cannot hear his command to the angels who have been waiting: *Go down and roll that useless stone away. Remain there and tell my Son's sisters and brothers the news.*

But perhaps we can begin to hear the terrified soldiers say, *What was that? An earthquake? Thunder? What are those shining ones by the tomb? Gods! It's open! What just happened? The body is gone! Our lives are forfeit! What can we do? Tell the religious leaders, make excuses… Run!*

And we can imagine those cunning Pharisees advising, *Take some money. Say you fell asleep. We'll cover for you.* We can hear the lie: *His disciples came and stole his body away!*

And in another building in the city, we can hear the women, up early, speaking softly. *Do we have everything? Look, the sun is finally rising.* We can imagine their sobs as they walk to the tomb in love and devotion, to place spices on the body of their dead friend.

They enter the garden, ready to work. *What will we do about the… wait… what?* The soldiers are gone. The stone has been moved. Perplexed and afraid, they enter the tomb. His body is not there—but angels are. The women bow to the ground. We can listen as one of these heavenly beings speaks:

> *Why are you looking for the living among the dead? … He is not here, but he has risen! Remember how he spoke to you … saying, "It is necessary that the Son of Man be betrayed into the hands of sinful men, be crucified, and rise on the third day"? (Luke 24:5-8)*

Listen to the women running back and telling their brothers what they have seen and heard. These men hear, but it seems like "nonsense" to most of them—typical hysterical women.

Listen as Peter and John run to the garden, just to be sure. Yes, the tomb is empty—but angels they do not see.

Listen now as Mary Magdalene continues her search for his body. She is alone and determined to find him. She weeps. The angels speak to her: "Woman, why are you crying?"

"Because they've taken away my Lord," she tells them, "and I don't know where they've put him" (John 20:13).

Watch now as she turns around and sees a man standing there. And hear the King's first words in his new world:

> *"Woman … why are you crying? Who is it that you're seeking?"*
>
> *Supposing he was the gardener, she replied, "Sir, if you've carried him away, tell me where you've put him, and I will take him away."*

Listen as King Jesus speaks her name:

> *Mary.*
>
> *My dear teacher!*

She falls on him and hugs him tightly. And he lets her.

And then he says, "Don't cling to me … Go to my brothers and tell them that I am ascending to my Father and your Father, to my God and your God" (v 17).

Listen as she weeps for joy and runs back to the place where they were staying, announcing to her brothers and sisters:

I have seen the Lord!

She proclaims his resurrection.

Keep on listening as later that day, the King appears to his ashamed and bewildered followers. In fear, they are hiding behind a locked door. But, like the stone, a locked door means nothing to him. He enters the room and says:

Peace be with you.

Hear him say to you, *Peace be with you. It is finished. My Father is now, and forever will be, your Father?* Listen as millions of saints in heaven proclaim—as you too will one day—"I have seen the Lord!" Listen as a vast number of people from every tribe and tongue and nation proclaim with a loud voice…

Salvation belongs to our God, who is seated on the throne, and to the Lamb! (Revelation 7:10)

Listen, and remember: *He lives.*

Reflect

Some church traditions have a practice of "Passing the Peace." To which Christian brother or sister could you say today, in faith, "Be at peace. All will be well"?

After Easter

Our Risen Shepherd

Monday

It Is I

"Have courage. It is I. Don't be afraid."
(Matthew 14:27)

Read Luke 24:13-48

On the same day that Mary Magdalene proclaimed the resurrection to Jesus' gathered followers, two disciples, one named Cleopas and the other unnamed—perhaps his wife, Mary—were traveling to Emmaus. Yes, they had heard about the empty tomb (Luke 24:22-24). But so what? They were hopeless. It was over. Unsure of what these reports meant (if they meant anything at all), they tried to make sense of it as they walked. Every step they took away from Jerusalem was a step closer to the darkness of unbelief.

So their good Shepherd rescued them. He would not let them just wander away. "What are you discussing together as you walk along?" (Luke 24:17, NIV) he asked. He let them talk. They thought they had understood the story and where it was heading, but then Jesus had been executed and it was over. The time had come to get back to real life and away from the dangers in Jerusalem.

These wandering sheep would not be abandoned by their Shepherd. Yes, he chided them for not understanding his story and retold it, but then, as he sat down at their table and broke bread, their eyes were finally opened (v 31). He was alive! Somehow… how could it be… it wasn't over. There was still hope. He vanished, and they headed back to Jerusalem to tell the story (v 32-35).

Later, while they were testifying about seeing him, the Shepherd walked through locked doors and "stood in their midst." He said, "Peace to you!" (v 36). What they were feeling at that moment was anything but peace. They were "startled and terrified" (v 37). You would have been, too. "Startled and terrified" would aptly describe us if someone we had watched die showed up at their funeral reception. Peace? Unimaginable. A resurrected body? Unthinkable.

There was another option, though. They thought they were seeing a ghost (v 37). That was the only other category they had for this kind of event. And it wasn't the first time they had mistaken him for one.

Once, Jesus had walked on the water to them as they struggled in a boat against a raging storm. "Have courage!" he said. "It is I. Don't be afraid" (Matthew 14:27). But they simply had no categories for a King like this. Ghosts? Yes, sure. A man who defied the laws of nature? No, absolutely not. And now, had he risen from the dead? Unlikely.

"Have courage! It is I. Don't be afraid."

"Peace."

"Have courage!"

"Hear my voice."

"It is I."

"Touch my wounds."

"Don't be afraid."

Their response? *Oh no! It's a ghost!*

Apparently it's easier to believe in ghosts than a resurrected King.

He continued to try to assure them. He showed them his deformed hands and feet, his body that had been mangled by spikes and spear. He invited them to come near, to touch him. He spoke peace to them and told them to have courage. They didn't need to struggle with doubt.

Even so, after all this, they still struggled. Yes, a little joy was breaking through, but they couldn't yet grasp that he was real. It was impossible. So he asked them,

> *Do you have anything here to eat? (v 41)*

Now, let me ask you a question: do you suppose Jesus was hungry? It's possible, but I doubt it. The point of his question was not to test their hospitality skills. It was to prove to them that he was really there, in the flesh. He ate broiled fish in front of them not to satisfy a physical need but because he wanted them to see who he was. He taught them:

> *These are my words that I spoke to you while I was still with you—that everything written about me in the Law of Moses, the Prophets, and the Psalms must be fulfilled. (v 44)*

As they still grappled to believe, he commissioned them. These confused, terrified cowards would be his witnesses. They had seen him and heard him and touched him (1 John 1:1-4). Now they were to tell his story, to proclaim "repentance for forgiveness of sins" to "all the nations" (Luke 24:47).

We too are commissioned. Tell it to the whole world. This story of forgiveness and welcome is for everyone because this is the friend of sinners for everyone. Have courage.

Reflect

Who will you tell? What courage will it require?

Tuesday

Follow Your Friend

"Do you love me more than these?"
(John 21:15)

Read John 21:1-19

Before we can get to Jesus' final encounter with Simon Peter, we have to remember the first time he met him. It was a scene just like the passage you read today, beginning on the seashore after a bad night of fishing. Jesus commanded the men who would become his disciples, "Put out into deep water and let down your nets for a catch," and soon it was full of fish (Luke 5:4). The miracle opened Simon's eyes and he saw Jesus, but he saw himself too: "Go away from me, because I'm a sinful man, Lord!" (v 8). "Don't be afraid," Jesus told him. "From now on you will be catching people" (v 10).

Simon Peter's self-awareness was a good place to start. Jesus knew what Peter was and also knew what he would become. Peter's only hope was the forgiveness and call of his King: *I will make you a person who gathers people to me.*

And now again, post-resurrection, after Peter had endured another frustrating night of fishing, Jesus commanded, "Cast the net on the right side of the boat" (John 21:6) and of course, the nets were so full of fish they were "unable to haul it in." When Peter realized it was the Lord on the shore, he "plunged into the sea" and swam in. Of course he did.

What had King Jesus been doing while the disciples were out fishing? Making breakfast. Before they had even brought in the fish they caught, Jesus already had a charcoal fire going with fish and bread on it. He knew his friends would be hungry, and once again he fed them: "Come and have breakfast" (v 12).

After they ate, Jesus took his friend aside and began to walk with him in private conversation down the shore. Jesus initiated the first conversation he had had with Peter since Peter had promised him that, even if everyone else's love failed and they deserted him, Peter would remain steadfast.

"Simon," Jesus asked him, "do you love me more than these?"

Do you still believe you are different than these men? Is your love stronger?

Surely Peter remembered his denial—"I do not know the man."

"Yes, Lord," he proclaimed, "you know that I love you."

"Feed my lambs," came the response from his Lord: *Care for my little ones.*

Again the question came: "Simon … do you love me?"

Again, surely Peter remembered his words that night: "I do not know the man."

"Yes, Lord … you know that I love you."

"Shepherd my sheep."

Care for my friends. Lay down your life as I did. It is not about your greatness. You are not above them.

A third time, the question was asked: "Simon … do you love me?"

How had Peter answered the last time a question came at him three times? "I swear I do not know the man."

This time, he answered, "Lord, you know everything."

Ah, finally. Finally Peter bends his knee to Jesus: *You know everything. You are right. And… "You know that I love you."*

"Feed my sheep," Jesus responded. He restored Peter to a place of ministry, but not because Peter had asked for forgiveness or had been open about his failures. Jesus initiated this three-fold confrontation about Peter's three-fold denial to bring Peter to where he should be.

You are God. You know everything.

You saw me that night. You see me as I am now.

You know I love you, but you also know how weak I am.

Ah. Finally. Now that Peter had seen his own failures and also Jesus' love for him, sinful as he was, he was fit to follow the King and fit to humbly care for others, people who were like him: weak and sinful.

He would be like his Savior: a friend of sinners.

Peter could not be a friend of sinners—he could not care for Jesus' flock—until he saw himself as one of them. And finally he had.

After telling Peter about the way he would follow him into a martyr's death, Jesus told him, "Follow me" (v 19).

My dear friends, here is your crucified and risen friend's word to you too. He knows who you are. He sees your weakness and failures. He also knows that you love him and that you are thankful that he is your friend. What he wants you to do and keep trying to do over and over is to get your eyes off the failures that make you hide and off the successes that make you think you are okay without him, and instead to humbly follow him, befriending other sinners.

Follow him.

And then, one day, perhaps soon, all manner of things will finally be well. You will walk with him by the crystal river and eat with him in pleasant pastures, where all your failures and the failures of others will be forgotten. In the meantime…

Follow him.

Reflect

Think back through this season of Lent. How has fixing your eyes on King Jesus as the friend of sinners changed you? How will you move forward?

Acknowledgments

To pastors Craig Marshall and Ryan Wentzel, who faithfully preached Christ to me during the creation of this book. I know it cost you. To Eric Schumacher and Colleen Ramser, friends in the battle who listen to and value the stories of others in the fight. You encourage me and make me brave. To Carl Laferton, for his invitation to write this devotional, and for his and Maggie Combs' work that made these devotionals readable. To my pals who read the unedited (gasp!) version of this work and let me know that I had achieved my goal because it reminded them of Jesus. Thank you! I have been so enriched by so many who graciously befriended this sinner.

And, of course, to my dear (growing) family. Your faithful love and patience have taught me so much about the faithfulness of Jesus. Thank you. And, as always, to my dear husband, Phil, who not only comforted me in my exhaustion and headaches and excused me from my obligations but also listened patiently as I read every devotion to him, day by day, and said, "That's good, dear." Your love has made me strong. Thank you always.

BIBLICAL | RELEVANT | ACCESSIBLE

At The Good Book Company we are dedicated to helping Christians and local churches grow. We believe that God's growth process always starts with hearing clearly what he has said to us through his timeless and flawless word—the Bible.

Ever since we opened our doors in 1991, we have been striving to produce resources that are biblical, relevant, and accessible. By God's grace, we have grown to become an international publisher, encouraging ordinary Christians of every age and stage and every background and denomination to live for Christ day by day and equipping churches to grow in their knowledge of God, their love for one another, and the effectiveness of their outreach.

Call one of our friendly team for a discussion of your needs or visit one of our local websites for more information on the resources and services we provide.

Your friends at The Good Book Company